Old Dime Box Stories

Niel Hancock

Old Dime Box Stories

FAST BOOKS

ISBN 978-0-9887162-6-1

Fast Books, P. O. Box 1268, Silverton, OR 97381

To the Reader

These little yarns are enough true to start some gunplay somewhere in the wrong circles, and therefore claimed to be unrelated to any person alive or dead. The country described is half geography, half mythography, and changing with every wind that blows down out of the Canadian border or up from the Gulf of Mexico.

Leaving tracks wasn't wise when you were crossing the Llano Estacado in front of a band of Comanches, and is not wise now, when the hostiles are not even as civilized as wild Indians once were. I'd rather take my chances with a fast horse and some common sense than try to navigate the shark-infested waters there are now, where bandits take a liking to gut-shooting people because it's entertaining to watch.

These passing scenes of life passed and passing are in compliance with the John Wayne/Gary Cooper/Roy Rogers Code.

Old Dime Box Stories

The Dragon Lines

Reaching for Tomorrow

Somewhere outside Roswell the storms drifted out over the Bottomless Lakes, the rain coming in sheets, and the lightning making the sky as brilliant as day for a millisecond or two, leaving a stranded ghost light to play across the roof of heaven. Miles of rolling prairie, full of the lost tales of lost travelers, met the eye in every direction.

It was a good place to think about the past and what it meant, and how I was going to have to find some cover for a while, to wait out the lightning and pouring rain. I had been here once with one of my first girlfriends in the late fifties and seen a Testarossa Ferrari run at the drags at the old airbase, where they had stationed B-47s. On the way home, someone had tried to put out a cigarette in the backseat ashtray, but it flared back to life some time much later, parked in the driveway of my grandfather's house. It was a summer night, and with my bedroom windows open, I smelled the seat covers burning and went out and doused the flames with a garden hose.

It was a long breakfast, knowing my grandfather would leave at any minute and crawl into the burned-plastic-smelling Ford to drive to work. My grandfather was a fair man, and I didn't die, and it cost me a month of grounding to see the ramrod-straight old man sink down into where the cushions should have been, his hat almost even with the window frame. He did see the humor of it, and it was funny, but I still did the time. Looking back now, it was also a testament to how well Fords were built in those years.

It was also outside Roswell that the UFO had crashed. The countryside was vast and wild, and the people who lived there were of a stiff-necked nature, not prone to active imaginations run amok. They loved the openness, and the space, and the gift

1

of nature, so it was hard to believe that a young ranch foreman should suddenly show up ranting about the alien ship and the small bodies that ended up in a blazing heap on a remote portion of his range. It was an event that was to thread its way into the warp and weave of my life over the years, right up until this very day, along with friends being disappeared, and the imprisonment of Tennessee Williams in a mausoleum in St. Louis.

I finally made it to the city limits and pulled into a motel, the hair on the back of my neck standing straight out from the electricity in the damp air. Unpacking the bike, I watched the night sky change, the black-on-black thunderhead rolling on away to the east, like a giant circus wagon lit by celestial lamps, accompanied by the distant rolling thunder. I had heard sounds like it before, from ARCLIGHT strikes in Viet Nam or the artillery batteries firing off their H&I missions into the sweaty night around the sprawling base.

It might have been a storm exactly like this that did in the aliens, whoever they were and wherever they were from. I've always liked to imagine that maybe they were relatives, coming back to check on their colonies on earth.

The night clerk at the motel told me about a small Mexican cafe nearby, and I went there, suddenly hungry, watching for signs of old ghosts from 1957, lost somewhere in the ozone and awakened by the noise of the storm.

Looking for the Trail

I was on my way to meet Bilbo Baggins when I got waylaid by the war. Jo Potts agreed to go out with my friend Bill Flowers, and there is a vague memory of a red and cream 1954 Ford Crown Victoria, but somehow it all ran off the Cosmic Highway, and the next thing I knew, there was a meteor shower, and then Dwight D. Eisenhower was old and slow and ready for retirement. World War II had been a handful, I guess, no wonder the old warrior was ready to hang it up. They were waiting for me, all hunkered down in their pin-striped suits and hundred-dollar haircuts, and had it not been for my knowing about Bilbo and the hobbits, I would've been a goner.

There's something to be said for the harsh times coming in the early going, and good old Delbert Lingneau kept up my spirits by pissing on the electrified fence, and Ursel Doran tickled my somewhat small store of hope by explaining to me the ultimate meaning of curling toes when two people were kissing. This lecture was delivered as we lay flat on a bedroom floor watching an unsuspecting drunken couple grope around one early dawn on the Panhandle of Texas. Life was like that when you were on the threshold.

In that same town, there was the most Secret of Secret, the Big Invisible, the Hole in the Ground that housed the deadliest of weapons, rows on rows of them, hundreds of feet beneath the surface of the earth. Palo Duro Canyon ran through it, and the name rolled off the tongue like a pretty Spanish filly, Amarillo. My friend Delvin Langdon and I had gotten falling down drunk one night at the Zen Bar and gone for a look at this mysterious, brooding place, because someone had been spinning yarns about it. A friend had done construction work on the underground complex, and at two in the morning it sounded like an excellent idea to go check on it ourselves.

Sedans full of very serious men with guns appeared, and it was much in our favor that we were simply college kids who had a snout full of booze. No one ever mentioned the fact that it was the ultimate top-secret sort of place, and that if you wanted your DNA intact, you would never dabble about near the joint.

We didn't get ventilated that night, but from what I know now, and what has been made public, we could easily have been shot as full of holes as an economy-sized colander. Delvin and I escaped that fate, but a Brahma bull by the name of Tornado caught up with him a few weeks later in Laramie, Wyoming, and I had to drive him all the way back to Texas with his right arm hung out the window, because he was in a body cast that went down to below his waist.

The cast was a mess by the time we got back to Amarillo, covered with all sorts of bugs that were attracted to the different crops that grew along the way, and to top off the catastrophic summer, we found out John Steinbeck and Charlie had stopped in for a drink or two at the Zen Bar, and Charlie had pissed on the pool table in the back.

That was what Casper the barkeep remembered most about the visit by the famous author, that his dog had taken a whiz on the pool table.

That all took place in the early sixties, when Pantex still hung on the Llano Estacado like the wisp of some lethal ghost. What was most frightening then, and now, is how invisible it all was. They assembled nuclear weapons there and still store them in those mysterious underground badger holes those mysterious construction workers dug, but it's almost like they never existed. The same mind disease that disappeared the unhuman bodies from the wreckage of the UFO outside Roswell, and gave us the best of every war from the American Revolution until now, and split mankind from mankind, kept the Pantex plant humming along behind their innocent-looking cyclone fences, as though they were out there making mobile homes or assembling automotive parts.

Georgia O'Keeffe lived in a house in Canyon, seventeen miles away, and painted the different moods of sunsets there in the early part of the century, before they brought their nuclear plague to live on the Great Pool Table. My grandfather and grandmother moved to that part of the country at about the same time. I grew up a hundred miles from the weapons plant, and never heard of what they did there until I was already caught up in the war in Viet Nam. On a day in early February 1968, I saw Amarillo listed on a big board of probable targets for any Russian or Chinese nuclear strike.

Amarillo! Right up there with the missile silos in the Midwest and the seaports on the Pacific and Atlantic.

Georgia O'Keeffe would have probably found something beautiful to paint out on the Pantex reservation, and I'm sure that over the years they paid a lot of taxes and employed a lot of locals. For all I know, I've had drinks with some of the guys who wore the little red buttons that monitored radiation. They might have hung out at the Zen Bar, and made bad jokes about Delvin's bug-splattered body cast, or bought rounds on Saturday nights. I wonder about them, just like I often wondered about the Vietnamese who went about our compound during the day, who wore black pajamas at night and were packing AK-47s. So well blended in, no hints or clues, and the never knowing was like a small stone in the back of your shoe.

The longer you walked on it, the more it began to bother you.

I was still in that neck of the woods in November of 1963 when President Kennedy was shot. My then wife and her parents were taking us to lunch when the radio announcer broke the news. My father-in-law's comment was that it was just what the Catholic bastard deserved. The awesomeness of that event filled up the back of the 1961 International Travelall, and it still haunts the party, like a hungry face at the window where there is a feast going on inside. My then wife did her part to propel me onto the trail of the Great Mystery by turning me in to my draft board in 1965, and I have learned to thank her for the wonderful gift she gave me. There is an old saying among those who know dragons, that the real meaning of their treasure is not that it sparkles or gleams in the light, but that it is the key to the Light, the Dragon Lore, which was just some old Chinese master's way of saying that to truly know the treasure of the dragon, you have to know that the measure of it is that you have succeeded in getting there, not the piles of baubles that lie at your feet.

When you stop to look back at something that seemed to be big in your life, you're often surprised at what a tiny dot on the horizon it actually was. Or it could be the other way as well. My old friend Charlie Norton, a cowboy who lived in Fort Hancock, Texas, could remember every horse he ever had, but he had trouble coming up with his first wife's name. He hated crowds and complained to me all the time that the country was getting too many people in it. That was in a town of maybe two hundred. My grandfather had felt that way too. When he finally built my grandmother a new house, he put it out on the prairie, on a plot of land that was nothing more than a grain sorghum field, and had a road graded out to it so the man who was building it could get his supply truck in and out. There was a five-foot-high cinderblock fence around the backyard, and as a young man, I would look out over the fortress wall at the vast expanse of bleak ocean and wonder how anyone could ever want to be there. That's before I understood the Dragon Lore, or had any hint at why the UFO that crashed outside Roswell had been in that particular part of the country.

The Native American knew all about the land, where the holy places were and what they all meant. When the white man came, he only understood the dragon's trinkets, and forgot the lesson of getting there. Even the aliens who were flying the ship that stormy night in 1947 understood, and I've often wondered if Charlie Norton wasn't out checking his herd at that same time, and might have seen another mystery moving across that vast part of heaven, to disappear into the ominous black thunderhead. From his corral, looking away off to the north and east, you could see all the way to the Canadian border, and it was not unlike Charlie to be out with his herd on stormy nights, talking to them to calm them, or just being out under that big sky he loved so much.

We talked about a lot of things when I would visit him. He didn't call them flying saucers or UFOs, but he described things he had seen over the years, traveling in and around the Chihuahuan desert. He didn't give them any more importance than what he might read in a sky that promised lightning storms. He would have been the young foreman that found the bodies from the crashed UFO, if those alien travelers had crashed on his spread instead of outside Roswell.

Charlie's thoughts on the Bottomless Lakes were this: if you had a few head of cattle to water on this side of the globe, then probably there was a Chinese rancher on the other, watering his cows there as well. Everything came down to nature and how to live with it.

He would have gotten along very well with Mrs. Rabbit, since they both understood how to go about dealing with a dragon trove.

Off the Front Porch

I was walking through the first exhibit of the Holocaust Memorial when the memory hit me of my Uncle Bob, an 82nd Airborne glider infantryman at Normandy. Fifty years or so is nothing when you stop to think of a Redwood, or Mount Everest, and even less of a number if you're only twenty-five years old, but there comes a point in everyone's life when half a century gives you long pauses for thought. Sometimes it looms in the distance like a spring thunderstorm, dark and ominous as it approaches,. At others, it's a memory that comes on you out of nowhere, and suddenly there you are, lost in some summertime-smelling night from your youth, the fire there again, the wonder of it all running through your veins, and a sweet sadness floods your thoughts then, of everything that was but is no more, and a great need to somehow put it all into perspective.

My friend Ed Snow lived in the Valley until he died and had assured me he had it in some sort of order. It means a 1955 jukebox which lived at the cafe in the Stonewall Jackson Hotel in San Benito, and an invisible line that you cross over somewhere below Hebronville, which puts you back into that time warp that was created when the UFO landed outside Roswell, New Mexico, back in 1947.

That's order from chaos and an explanation for anything that needs explaining, especially all those loose-ended sticker-patch items that no one is ever able to explain satisfactorily.

Like whatever happened to the apple-cheeked kid from Moline who drank warm beer and sang little Mexican songs in the barracks? What was it about coming home from Viet Nam alive that killed him months later? Or the long, empty nights between 1968 and the dedication of the Vietnam memorial in Washington in 1982? I watched the Armed Forces Network in

Viet Nam, on the news of the deaths of Martin Luther King and Robert Kennedy, and put that right up alongside the fact that my commander-in-chief was also a stockholder in Brown & Root, an outfit that was making a killing (excuse me) in Viet Nam. If there was ever a doubt about the double-sided nature of the explanation of U.S. policy in a war-torn nation, there was always the truth of it when you were there on the ground, watching the people of the country who needed your help, balanced against the huge meat-grinder of an operation that was fueled with lives of everyone caught up in its path, leaving behind odd traces of its passing in the brass bearing the imprint of Winchester Arms, or the stench of Dow Chemical hanging in the exotic tropical air. I used to wonder about the meaning of it all, and decided that I was never angry with small brown people in black pajamas, or even the NVA, but rather had a bone to pick with people like Robert McNamara and Henry Kissinger, or the faceless heads of corporations who grew fat on the lives of an entire generation of young men who were snatched up from their I-like-Ike lives and deposited into a monstrous firestorm which still has not seen an end.

That, and the irony that we were caught up in a crusade to help the Republic of South Viet Nam, and in the end, we packed up and left. We won every engagement, yet lost the war. And I have grown grateful for having fought for a lost cause, because I have never known the terrible guilt and confusion that comes from being caught up in a celebration of something so dreadfully permanent as the horrible scars that war leaves on everyone who has been in it. There are things too terrible to tell, and it cannot reach those who have not been initiated.

I think I hear faint echoes of the late sixties from the likes of No Doubt and Busta Rhymes, and the cacophony of voices such as Kurt Cobain or Nine Inch Nails. Everything changes, yet nothing changes. Bruce Springsteen sang the title song from his album "Born in the USA," which summed up a feeling as close as you could get about the experience of Viet Nam, just like the music with a nice heavy beat that became an anthem for the young soldiers who were described as rock-'n'-rollers with one foot in the grave. My mind strays to a scene in the Seattle/Tacoma airport when I flew back to The World. There was a sea of uniforms of all descriptions coming and going, and the very odd sensation that I had of somehow ending up in an exact replica of the United States of America but in another galaxy, somewhere far away from where I had departed.

I might as well have been aboard that ill-fated UFO that crashed in New Mexico for all the feeling of warmth and security at being "home." My family looked familiar, and all my friends had their same faces on, but that was it. They weren't changed, but I was. They were on their side of the fence looking at me from their picket-fence, academic lives, wondering what had happened to the person they used to know.

And there was no way to tell them. In their way, they meant well and were afraid, or meant well and looked the other way. I had many suggestions about how to get my life back in order. My mother thought a stint at the Bin would do it. That's what I always called her combo of psychiatry and psychology. You could take your matching bedspread and curtains and just hole up until they found the right pill to make you better. My friend Ed Snow and my mother were great telephone conspirators, matching stories of prescriptions that were good, and those which weren't. I drove her to the coast where the Bin was not long after I came home from the war, and sat in the office of her favorite doctor, waiting for how they would try to phrase the sentence.

"So Niel, I hear you just got back from Viet Nam," he said when we were alone, and he promptly pulled open the bottom drawer of his desk, where he retrieved an almost full fifth of Wild Turkey. He poured out two water glasses full of the whiskey and pushed one across to me.

"Ching ching," I said, saluting him, and downed it, feeling the rolling heat sweep all the loose ends of things from beneath the bed in the dark back into their hiding places.

He told me I could probably use a little time to unwind, and that it might be a good idea to come see him sometime soon. I thanked him and went around the corner to the liquor store and bought my own fifth of Wild Turkey and sat out on the beach all night, watching the Gulf turn and roll, singing its old sea-chantey songs, and slowly easing my thoughts toward sleep.

A storm had rumbled up out of the Gulf one September, around the same date I was there, but that storm was in 1900, and it wiped the place clean. I watched in the early dawn light, wondering what that must have felt like. From stories and pictures, it looked to be about the same as a two-day operation in Viet Nam, only Nature always does it so much better.

If you want to have your attention gotten, there's nothing for it like a Gulf blow, with winds that have been getting bigger and meaner all the way from the coast of Africa.

A good way to get you moving, much like being drafted, or hightailing it for rough country to get out of the way of angry citizens, or being hungry in a place where there is no food. My propulsion had come in the form of an irate and vengeful soon to be ex-wife who turned me in to my draft board after our divorce in 1965.

When she found out I was going to Viet Nam, she wrote to tell me she hoped I'd lose my legs.

I rode that horse for pity for a long time, until I stopped to take a look at some of the things I'd done that would make her feel that hateful toward me. All she'd ever wanted was to work as a fashion merchandiser and live a regular life, and she was stuck with an alien breed, who hung out with writers and poets and biker riff-raff, and thought that the life of a starving artist was as good a thing as Delvin Langdon wanting to ride mad Brahma bulls.

Charlie Norton never did any rodeoing, because to his mind it was all a lot of fluff started by men who would never be able to make it as a real cowboy. He also never had a regular life, and the wives he had must have spent a lonely lifetime, living with a familiar stranger.

My ex never realized what a gift she had given me, and I didn't either, until I'd had a chance to look at it all from some distance.

A Chinese gift wrap. That's what I call things that on the initial glimpse look to be something from a diabolical torture plot. It comes in descending-sized boxes, from big to small, then smaller, then smaller still.

Every man gets the dragon he deserves, they say, not to punish, but to prepare you for the day when you will need the strength you've gained from the struggle.

Whoever said life was supposed to be easy?

It helps when you find out that we're lost out here in the wilderness, trying to find our way back. Not to the place I thought I was returning to when I came back from Viet Nam, but to that other destination, where everyone gets to unpack their sea bags and sit a while out on the Big Guy's front porch.

Things like that make sense, but only after you've been gone for a good long while, and there are a dozen beasties at the door, and your gun's jammed.

The Cosmic Two-by-Four.

Travel is the true state of the heart and one of the last pure impulses that drive us, like the birds flying south in winter.

We just have to learn how to listen.

The Rearview Mirror

Everyone has a different feeling when they start out for the Sacred Mountain, but it always begins one day when you least expect it. Time and circumstances gang up on you, and off you go, sometimes with not even so much as an overnight bag. Your only options seem to be what sort of means you're going to use to get there.

I had a small stuffed animal once, of a character from *The Book Of Seven Arrows*, Little Mouse, a very small Great Being who went to find the Sacred Mountain. My small stuffed critter made his own way there by moving to L.A. and getting a Ferrari.

It takes all kinds.

And all roads to lead home. It's a matter of recognizing the territory and knowing how to read the clues. My grandfather's friend Mooch Crane always said the smartest man in the world was the first man who looked at a lobster and thought he could eat it. Mooch was not a Down East lobsterman but a cotton farmer in the Panhandle of Texas.

Some people take longer than others, through no fault of their own. They park in one place, look around, and decide that's it. I hit the ground running and haven't stopped since, although at the time I had no idea where I was going. My grandmother would call my grandfather at his office to tell him I had escaped, and he would leave work and drive around until he found me. Even when I was told my behavior was killing my grandmother, and I was whipped with a switch from the pussy willow tree in our backyard, I just couldn't stop myself. When the door would open I'd be gone.

That was age five. It's gotten worse over the years.

I hadn't discovered what exactly it was in me that would

13

listen to that lonesome whistle of the great steam engines that used to run the Santa Fe Railroad, those gigantic black beasts that would hiss and roar as they took on water at the depot. I'd lie in my bed electrified as they began to huff and chug and slowly gain speed on their way to some wonderful place that I could not even dream of yet.

The starched white Snow Geese who lived behind me on Back Bay in Virginia affected me the same way. The sight of them circling and gathering together their flock for their long trip to the tundra, and their voices as they called and talked to each other, also talked to my heart.

And when you're open to that, magic things begin to happen.

Petey the Snow Goose turned out to be one of those unexplained things that get dropped on you when you least expect it. He'd been wounded by a hunter. I found him holed up in a stand of rushes across from the house I was living in then. He wasn't happy about being moved, but I got him to a vet, who set his broken wing but told me there wasn't much chance of the bird living long enough to fly again. It's what happens, he explained, when a flyer gets grounded.

You get depressed because you can no longer fly, and then you just stop wanting to live.

The lesson as regards our human condition was not lost on me, because I had gotten onto a part of the Trail by then, and knew that in the highest forms of yoga, the soul is referred to as a bird longing to return to the sky.

Kenny Kinslow was a pal of mine in those days, and between the two of us, along with help from a dozen or so others, we set out to rehabilitate Petey, so that when the spring came, he'd be able to make it back up north with his family. After he was well enough to get the splint off his wing, and was given a clean bill of health in that area, we began to take him on walks out into the Back Bay marshes, where he could visit with the flock he had come with, and with all the rest of his kind as well. It surprised

14

me at first to learn that they travel in families, and stay with that group as long as they live. They also take a mate for life.

The strip of road that ran past my house was bordered on one side by the dunes that ran down to the beach, and on the other was Back Bay, a vast marshland that was home to all the migrating birds from every flyway over Virginia. Beyond the bay, the woods began. We had our flying lessons on the road, for it was a summer resort community, and after Labor Day, the local population dropped to almost nothing. Kenny and I took turns being "Mom," running up and down that road flapping our arms and making goose noises, trying to get Petey to exercise and maybe try to test his recovering wing. The doctor who'd worked on Petey assured us sadly that it was a lost cause, but neither one of us was willing to buy that. Kenny was a two-tour 'Nam medic with an intense way of relating to anyone and anything, and it must have amazed and dumbfounded the remaining residents to witness our afternoon bird-school antics.

Petey would follow us, but he never made an effort to fly. It went on that way all through the late fall and early winter. By the time spring arrived, the great flocks of geese on Back Bay were beginning to grow restless, and to practice their departure. We were growing more desperate by the day, as one by one, the formations of the beautiful white birds would circle out around over the dunes, up into the sun, calling, always calling, with those sounds that made your heart leap and every nerve strain toward the dome of blue sky, pointing away home.

Petey by now followed us like a pet dog and was quite affectionate. He slept on the back porch or on the dock in a canal at the back of the house, and I would hear him talking to his friends all through the night. As time drew on, and a number of the groups had circled above us and gone, Petey began to grow agitated and walk up and down the side of the canal, honking with a heart-rending noise. Kenny and I made a vow that if he couldn't get airborne, we would drive him to the Canadian border and smuggle him home.

Day by day the number of Snow Geese on Back Bay dwindled, and then there were only the small groups of the last-to-depart. Winslow and I were working with Petey on the road on a Sunday in April, when almost all the bay was deserted. Where the beautiful talkative birds had been, there was now nothing but vast, empty stretches of marshland. Petey was hopping along behind us with an odd sort of gait, running a few steps, then hopping. It was the first time he had managed to make any attempt to really use his old skills, and we ran back and forth down the dune road until we were both exhausted. A flock of geese had flown out low over the beach, far out to sea, and circled back, their honks and calls fading into the distance, then coming back again. They buzzed us there on the road, and it reminded me of a flight of Phantoms once, off Highway One in Viet Nam. Petey was beside himself. Without thinking, he started off down the road to follow his brothers, running awkwardly, stumbling once, regaining his balance by spreading out his wings.

As Kenny and I watched in amazement, he moved forward a little more, and with one simple motion caught himself and rode up the wind's back, as simple as you please. With a few more powerful strokes, he was airborne, riding up the blue edge of the beach sky toward his friends, who were waiting and calling to him.

The two gangsters below cried and hugged each other until a car came, its occupants looking at us strangely, then hurrying on, afraid we were wild-eyed lunatics escaped from our Chinese Tuxedos. We watched as Petey fell into the familiar V formation, and then the group came back toward us, low over the dunes. As they passed, they wheeled up into the sun, and for a moment or two in time, their white bodies turned a brilliant gold. They flashed past, far out to sea, then higher up coming back, then flew by, calling out in celebration. We could hear Petey's excited honk above all the rest, and we waved and waved, until they vanished from sight.

We were still waving for some time after they were gone, our voices too unsteady to try to speak. In a while, the tide began to roll in, coming slowly up the beach in that regular motion the ocean has as it's breathing, and we walked slowly back up the road to the house, full of our own thoughts.

It was very quiet that first night after Petey was gone, and the Bay was deserted, with only the marsh birds left. I always wonder about Petey in the fall, when he and his brothers would be coming south. That longing, that feeling of going south, beats as steady and true in us at it does in the Snow Geese, and it's the first small hint we have of the desire to go Home.

That all probably had something to do with why I was bitten with the motorcycle bug one summer when I first started work as a teenager at O.C. Pullem's Gulf Service Station. It was the summer after my freshman year in high school, when a sailor being transferred from San Diego to Baltimore came through town on a maroon and silver Bonneville Triumph. There are those moments in your life that you'll remember, for they're etched forever in your mind's eye, like your first crush, that first cruel wound of losing it, then the freedom of flight out into the big world, away from your family's apron strings. If you have the luck, you'll keep adding to that list as your times run by.

Just like crossing trails with Petey. And there's something about a motorcycle trip that reminds me of that feeling I got listening to those Snow Geese calling as they were riding up that big patch of sky. It's different than being on any other form of transportation, other than a sailboat, or maybe a horse. Flying is probably the same, but I never learned how, for some reason. Maybe I read the old myth once too often, of Icarus, who made himself wings. He used beeswax, and it melted when he flew too high, too near the sun. Funny how appropriate that old story is even now. I look out over my upstairs verandah, and straight back into the mirror, and see that first bike. It was a 1957 Harley-Davidson Sportster, a deep red with cream, and lots of chrome. I'd never seen anything like it. Nadine, the daughter of the dealer, rode one just like it, only hers was white. Everyone at the bike shop was totally smitten with Nadine, but she only had eyes for an airman from the base, who was from somewhere on the East Coast and rode a British bike. This was all in the same small town only a hundred and ten miles from where the unfortunate space travelers were lost, and I could always somehow identify with the feelings of loneliness and isolation they must have had before they went down, just by growing up in that vast wilderness of endless sky and unending prairie. Every pilgrim who ever ventured out across those uncharted miles was wired up the same as the men who flew the ships from NASA, except that they walked or rode wagons or horses, but the emotional landscape would be the same.

Going where no one had gone before. Great dangers, from rocket explosions on the pad, or hostile Indians coming to take your scalp, or just simply drifting in space. On earth it might be starvation, lack of water, wild animals, or disease. The great debate of whether one is afraid of death, or of the process of dying, does it hurt, is it peaceful? Is there really a bright white light that appears? All questions that answer themselves, given enough time, and motorcycles seemed to be a natural vehicle to help me sort out that mystery.

Walter Rabbit used a sailboat, and Charlie Norton went horseback. My grandfather used his business, a bank, of all things, as his magic carpet. It was the great open prairie that brought it all into focus. When you're surrounded by such a vast open space, it's necessary to make boundaries, to somehow hold yourself down onto the earth. The West Texas Overtow Theory is that unless you stand next to a tree, or house, or car, you'll be sucked away into that Great Maw. In looking at hundreds of old photographs taken in and around my hometown, I can scientifically support that theory. Mooch Crane, one of my grandfather's domino partners, always called it the Slip Shift. You ride around on a tractor on a section of land all day from sunup to sundown, or stay out on your cow pony looking for strays, and you begin to get a little light in the bottom, he said. Start to float right on up.

He recounted a story one of his friends had told him of a man from Muleshoe who went off on wheat harvest one year, and somewhere up in Kansas or Nebraska, he couldn't recall exactly which, for it's all the same stretch of prairie, the fellow got tired and forgot to keep his Slip Shift in gear, and he drifted right on up out of the cab of that John Deere combine and vanished. They had to come back empty-handed and tell his wife and kids he was gone. They never heard another word. Mooch said the man's family packed their truck and went off in search of him, and as far as he knew, they had disappeared too.

I've tried to use the Slip Shift on more than one occasion in my life, but I've come to believe it only works in that vast prairieland that runs through the center of the country, from the Panhandle of Texas on up through the Great Plains to the Canadian Provinces above.

Petey the Snow Goose understood that and tried to teach us as best he could, but we still need more rehearsal, just like running up and down that road in Sandbridge, Virginia, trying to remember how we learn to fly.

The Bilbo Baggins Song

Looking back, it's come to my attention that somebody might get lost, if they don't know the signs on the Trail. I mentioned Bilbo Baggins to a person under forty, and they had that puzzled look that tells you you're speaking a foreign language. Probably what one of the aliens might have sounded like to the young ranch foreman who found them out there on the edge of his spread in the New Mexican desert that night in 1947. Some have said it was an experimental aircraft that had strayed off course from the testing grounds in Alamogordo, but that story never washed with anyone. More likely, when they set off the Big One out there at Trinity Site, it signaled some life-form on one of the other planets, and they came down to have a look-see at what we'd been up to here on Earth.

Charlie Norton thought that made sense. He'd felt the ground tremble when they fired off the test bombs at Trinity Site and said his cattle had acted strangely. They were uneasy and jumping around to hear what it had been, but all he could make out was what he described as a gunshot in a grain silo, that had echoed and echoed for hours afterward. I tried to imagine what could have caused that, and then remembered the Carlsbad Caverns, and the Ogalalla Aquifer, and the vast underground river in that region. Charlie thought there were probably spirits that lived down there, and that it had upset them, because he could still hear faint echoes, even years later. When I asked him about it, he told me a story about a young cowboy named Elkins he'd known in the thirties. He was riding for a rancher outside Carlsbad at the time. One night in a thunderstorm, he was trying to head off a stampede that had started from a lightning strike when he rode off a rise in the dark and was thrown from his horse. He ended up in a depression covered by heavy underbrush. Trying to claw his way to the top and remount his horse, he slipped and fell back, and instead of stopping at the bottom of the hole, he tumbled on though a narrow rock cave mouth and skidded and bumped his way more than a hundred feet. It was pitch black, and the cowboy was sure he'd landed in a rattlesnake den, but when he lit a match to try to find his way out, he began to realize he was in some sort of vast chamber. A very faint breeze kept blowing his matches out. He knew he'd have to find a way up, and he promised himself he'd come back in the daylight to try to discover more of the huge sinkhole he'd stumbled upon. His thoughts were that there might be some of his cows trapped there, so he clawed and climbed, and finally got back topside, and went home to the ranch to tell his foreman. He left a piece of rag there on the bushes at the top to mark the spot, so they'd be able to find it the next day.

Charlie said Elkins went back as planned and found the spot, but when he lowered himself back down with a kerosene lantern, the blackness swallowed the light before it got more than a foot or two from him. He'd walked quite some way from the place he'd entered. It was then he began to realize the vastness of the cavern. He could hear the sounds of water from somewhere, but he'd started to be afraid he couldn't find his way back to the opening he'd come through. He finally found his voice, and hollered out, not knowing what to expect. What came back was terrifying to the young cowboy. His voice was swallowed up in the darkness, but the echo of it kept ringing and ringing, until he was so spooked he scrambled right up and out of the hole, and just sat there for some time, trying to imagine what it could mean. When he put his ear to the ground, it seemed like he could still hear the echo of his voice rattling on, further and further away. His boss told him to fence the sinkhole if the opening was big enough for any of their livestock to fall into, and to forget it otherwise.

But Charlie said his friend couldn't forget it. He kept

spending time out there, carrying more and more lengths of rope, then rolls of twine, but he'd still gotten no nearer to an end of the cavern. Because there was fresh air, he'd taken to putting down torches in the ground, and going on further, drawn by the immense space of the place, but he'd gotten afraid he'd go so far he wouldn't be able to find his way back. He had to be content to know that he'd found an entrance to a cavern so vast and long it must be part of one big underground maze, and an undiscovered part of the great caverns at Carlsbad.

He discovered he wasn't the only one to have found the sinkhole. On his last trip, he stumbled over something in the flickering lantern light. When he looked closer, it was a large rock with some distinctive marks on it, and when he studied it more carefully, his heart jumped up into his throat. It was some sort of Indian writing, with pictures and words. There were arrowheads and a few ceramic pots, and when he explored around a bit more, he moved some of the stones that had been piled in a heap and picked up a wrist bone, complete with a hand.

Not bothering to retrieve his torches, or his rope and twine that afternoon, he never went back.

"Indians," said Charlie, squinting his eyes up until you couldn't see them anymore. "They knew about those places and used them." He would usually roll a cigarette then, to punctuate his words. "They had a word for places like that. Means where God lives." He pointed out the desert mountains rising in the distance, off across the Rio Grande. "They thought He lived there, too."

"Whatever happened to your friend?"

"Elkins? Enlisted in early '42. He'd been out chasing strays when they bombed Pearl Harbor. He didn't even know there was a war going on for days."

Charlie looked out to the mountains to the west. "I got a letter from his sister. Said he'd been killed somewhere out in the Pacific. Place called Gaudalcanal." He shook his head and wiped the sweatband of his hat with a bandana. "I'm kinda like an Indian when it comes to being buried. Wouldn't want to be so far from my old huntin' grounds. Don't think I'd rest easy."

I thought about that when he said it back then, and I was thinking about it as I sat in the cafe watching the storm. It made me wonder about whoever was on that alien ship, and where they were from, and if anyone ever knew what happened to them.

The cave Elkins stumbled on turned out to be a monster. They still haven't been able to find an end to it, and they've already gone fifty miles. I wondered, too, if the young cowboy's fate was caused by disturbing the sleep of the Indian he'd found there. That's the thing about starting to wonder about that stuff, your mind just takes off on its own.

My friend Pat Boatwright came across an unmarked grave when he was diving in the Bahamas in the early seventies. The law was that when you came on a site like that, you would mark the date and put your name on it. That was the old law. A few days later, another person, not knowing that old maritime code, found the grave with Pat's name on it and they reported his death to the Coast Guard. He had a hell of a time convincing anyone he was alive for quite a while after that. They finally had an official hearing and called Pat in, and he was glad to report that the rumor of his death had been greatly exaggerated.

Pat did admit that it was somehow freeing to know you were already dead and buried, so you get on with your life with renewed interest in everything.

Charlie Norton just vanished into the Chihuahuan desert. Two of his vaqueros came to the house where he was laid out for visitation before the funeral and got him. He had never wanted to be buried "in a mob" and had made his own arrangements. Whenever I'm out that way on a trip, I go by the cemetery where they have his marker to say hello, knowing Charlie's somewhere out in the vast desert, resting easy, next to one of his old favorite cowponies.

Bilbo Baggins was a hobbit who loved pipeweed and spinning good yarns. He was a free spirit and had an itch to travel now and then. He understood dragon troves and knew a thing or two about friendship. There's a legend of the Marfa Lights, which people have been seeing for years and years, but no one has ever been able to explain what they are. I have always thought they were campfires, with Indians and hobbits and cowboys like Charlie and Elkins sitting around under those vast heavens, smoking and talking about the kinds of secrets you always wanted to know about, delighted with the travel tales, no longer confined to just one range to ride.

You get to the oddest places, once you hear about Bilbo and Charlie, and the next thing you know, you're off looking for the Marfa Lights, or stepping down off your own front porch step to wherever it is you have always wanted to go.

Trips always start like that.

And you never know where you'll finish up, except that deep down, you know you're on the Road, and that you can be sure you have a place at the fire out here with all your other friends.

Top Shunk's Always Sound Advice

From the first day I met Sergeant Frederick J. Shunk, I knew there had been a flap in the sail of fate that blew us around in this world, and somehow or other, it was one of those events, like the feeling you get when you cross over a Dragon Line and get chills up and down your backbone and the sure knowledge in your gut that some things were just meant to be.

Sitting over my enchiladas in that Mexican cafe in Roswell, I watched the early evening storm blow by, seeing the raindrops against the window and hearing the now diminishing claps of thunder fading into the darkening night. In between the waitress coming to bring more coffee, and the pecan pie with ice cream, the film slipped a notch, and I was back at Charley Company HQ, sitting in the orderly room with Top Shunk, listening to the faintly audible rumble of small arms and mortars from away in the direction of the Newport River Bridge. He had been talking about his farm in Georgia and the fishing we'd do once we got back to The World.

Top had been a Japanese prisoner of war in World War II, then stayed on for Korea, and in the twilight of a long and honorable career, there he was in Viet Nam. He told me he didn't know any better, and that he couldn't stand desk jobs. Our commanding officer knew Top was the secret of staying alive, so we were luckier than some that way. Professional soldiers are a strange lot, warriors who hate war, and they have eyes that have seen things that are beyond the realms of ordinary men. You either loved or feared a man like Top. There was also the feeling that if you were with him, nothing could ever happen to you, like a luck piece that worked, or a writ from God that you would always be safe around him.

It had been the truth, and Top's best advice on the day the

truck came to take me away to the plane for The World was the same he'd always given, "Be very careful, do the best you can, and always keep a fresh round in the chamber."

Years later, the red-haired girl I was with at the time didn't want anything to do with Fort Gordon, Georgia, and I missed saying adios to him. He retired, and that pulled his plug, it seems. He was dead of cancer in four months, although I often wonder whether or not his ghost might not be hanging around a battalion orderly room there, keeping the new troopers in line and squaring away the young officers.

Top and some of the rest of the mob had hashed over what it all meant and where it all might be going. I'm sitting here down the road a bit from all that time ago, and I can see he always had kept it in perfect focus. If it was there, do it. Trendy sayings like "Be here now" came to pass later on, but Top was into it all his life, and he spread the word to anyone who came into his bailiwick. I remember sitting listening to a then popular song at the NCO Club, "We Gotta Get Out of This Place," wondering what the hell had happened in the Cosmic Script, when Top walked in, talking about fishing in Georgia and worrying about two young soldiers who had come into the company as replacements. We drove around that night in a gun-jeep and visited the newbies at their posts. They were wide-eyed and nervous, talking very fast and clutching their weapons tightly. Top talked about the patience that fishing requires and questioned them about where they were from and where they'd done their training, slowly putting them at ease, although the night was growing darker, with that two o'clock smell that was a combination of tropical heat and garbage and sweat, mixed in with the sticky-sweet smell fear makes. Tiger and Foo, the Coke boys who sold soft drinks to G.I.s, hadn't made their rounds yet. I warned the new troops about them and admonished them to buy something from the two young Vietnamese, who talked of going to school in the United States and wanted to learn to play baseball. They supported their mother and two young sisters after their father was killed in the unrest of 1964, and could tell you the capitals of all the states at a rapid pace. Top liked the two small hustlers and said we could have used more of them to boost our chances of a successful operation.

Sitting there in the cafe in the stormy Southwestern town, I thought back on that vast city of Saigon in the monsoon and wondered whatever had happened to those new troops, and to Tiger and Foo. There was a feeling then of being swept up in a great wave, slowly building and building at sea. Where it stopped, no one would know, or begin to understand the full monstrousness of it. We still had not seen the end of it, even as I sat finishing my coffee in the Mexican restaurant in Roswell, where the Sky Riders had crashed.

I must have been a bad night for whoever was aboard that craft, just as it had been the worst of nights for those two new troops, the FNGs, sitting in that first tropical night in Viet Nam, lost and far away from everything they had ever known or found familiar. Tiger and Foo would have filled their heads with terrible stories, recounting endless incidents to the new men. They were known at the Battalion for having the best information available.

When Tiger and Foo said beaucoup VC, you had better be cleaning your weapons and carrying a couple more bandoliers of ammunition.

They called Tet of '68 right on the button, although no one higher up would believe that two Coke boys could have such hard evidence of an operation of the size they were describing. I thought about the young ranch foreman and his information about the UFO and had to laugh in my coffee. No one would have believed him either, except that there were small non-human bodies to be carried away and studied, just like there was the whole aftermath of the Lunar New Year in 1968 to be reckoned with, right up until the end of the war in 1975 and beyond, ticking still, even as I sat there in that booth in a town

27

in New Mexico, watching the last of the thunderstorm dying away in the distance, listening to echoes of another time.

Very Affordable Mary

As far as I know, she never told anyone but my friend Arty her real name, so we took to calling her Mary, and it stuck. She was very beautiful, with jet black hair and honey-colored skin, born in 1946 to a French Legionnaire and a Vietnamese mother who had been forced into prostitution after her lover was sent back to France. He had promised to return for her, and Mary was convinced he would have but for the unfortunate war in Algeria, which killed him. The mother had worked for a time as a maid in the French Embassy befriended a high-ranking official there, and in time made good use of her connections to the upper strata of the population of Saigon. When the French left in 1954, she was the mistress of a personal secretary to the new regime in power, and that was the way things stood in 1967, when I arrived in-country. Her mother was half-owner of a high-class house on Tu Do Street, which was patronized by the upper crust of representatives of all the governments that had interests in Southeast Asia. The silent partner was a wealthy Australian looking for good ways to make his money work for him in the wide-open boomtown that was Viet Nam in those early years. He furnished her with access to round-eyed girls. They were paid from $500 on up per night, which was beyond the reach of most of the G.I.s, but not for field-grade officers, or visiting dignitaries.

Our unit drank free soft drinks when we were on duty, and booze in the salon when we were off, providing an umbrella of security in an official capacity, since we were charged with protecting all American personnel and installations in the city of Saigon, and the place was always full of Americans. Professional courtesy never extended as far as cut-rates on the girls working there. It was enough to be able to sit in the bar and talk with them and dream about what might have been.

Mary's mother took a liking to my friends and me, which would eventually lead to the bizarre affair of the murdered Colonel. We found the company delightful, and her daughter became like our own sister. We would stop by at all hours to make sandwiches in their kitchen or check out a new arrival from Australia. The girls from Down Under would work a short six-month tour and go home with enough money stashed to buy a new car or make a wedding dowry. Some of the girls bought houses for their parents, or sent siblings to school, or opened businesses of their own back home. We were in love with all of them and kept pictures of them around the hooch, which was a special kind of torture, like a condemned man allowed to see everything he was never going to be allowed to have before being hanged.

The war was our gallows, and no one ever knew when the trapdoor was going to be sprung. If you were lucky, you were just dead. If you had no luck, you would be horribly maimed and forced to live on for years, like being gut-shot and sitting down to slowly feel yourself bleed to death inside. Things like the pretty round-eyed girls in the house on Tu Do Street helped keep you sane enough to survive long enough to maybe survive, or the three-inthe-morning thoughts of a convertible Mustang, with a pocketful of mustering-out pay, and nowhere to go but to the next party when you rotated home to The World.

There was a backlash to the insanity of living in a combat zone, even if it was exotic and had a French-speaking society, as we were to find out when the Colonel from the East Coast finally slipped over the edge one night just after our graveyard-shift watch came on duty. He had been pestering Mary's mother for weeks to sell her to him, promising to take her back to America and make an honest woman of her. Mary's mother was a good businesswoman, but she was a mother, too, so she sold him Mary by the night. That only whetted his appetite for her, and he began to come to the house every night after he was off duty, buying her when she was not already with someone else, or standing outside the room where she had taken her client, brooding and pacing like a wounded animal. Mary's mother complained to us, and Top came with us one night in early January 1968 to try to talk some sense into the Colonel.

Top was diplomatic and knew many of the senior officers in Viet Nam from his prior tours of duty, and the talk seemed to have done some good. The Colonel stayed away, unless he was actually with Mary, and the clock ticked on, second by second, as it often did when it was all too quiet, and you could sometimes hear the blood coursing through your veins, if it was very late and very dark. Sometimes you could also hear the heart of your enemy, ever so close and full of the blackest hatred, which would wake you up out of a fitful sleep and have you looking for your weapon, to cradle it like a teddy bear or some old, lost object from a distant childhood, when you woke to imagined monsters under the bed.

There were no imagined monsters in Viet Nam, just the reality of flitting shadows and hints of danger, with sudden violent explosions that lit up the sky and turned the world into a dreadful nightmare with far-reaching echoes that came and receded like waves on a storm-driven sea. The sights and smells of that time are never far away, and the mind plays out its own tapes on its VCR sometimes when the temperature is hot and muggy and a garbage truck rolls past, the diesel mixing in with the pungent aroma of the debris people discard.

Arty took Mary's secret to his grave when he suicided a few months after he left Viet Nam, and I never knew if she or her mother got out of Saigon before it fell, although I have that subtle feeling inside that they probably somehow survived. Any one of us would have taken Mary back to The World with us, but she was a beautiful enigma, and no matter how hard you tried, you could never quite touch her. You could lose yourself in her smile, and her eyes were as dark and deep as the smiles of the monks we would see on the road, watching us pass by on our mechanical armored elephants. I have always thought the reason Mary told Arty her name was that she saw the death in him and knew her secret would be safe. They had a bond between them, as only the doomed can have, sacred and inviolate, a song from a place so secret that no one else hears.

The Colonel also had a secret, and it was kept as well. When the young Marine officer shot him, his mind was gone. He had kicked open the door of the room and dragged Mary out of the bed, his eyes blood-red, ranting about saving her from the fires of hell. He was also carrying his regulation sidearm, waving it around, and fired off a round through the ceiling. In the dark and the insanity of the moment, the well-disciplined young soldier protected himself as he had been taught and put two .45 caliber rounds through the middle of the Colonel, killing him almost instantly. We got Mary's mother's frantic phone call just before two o'clock in the morning.

That was in the early morning hours of January 31st, 1968.

Tet had kicked off in the usual way, and the fireworks were going off in every part of town, lighting the sky with incredible displays and making it almost impossible to talk. The Colonel had gone to take Mary's mother a present of black market cash to buy Mary, which she refused. That's when he went upstairs and was killed.

In another few minutes, the city of Saigon erupted into a fiery maelstrom that did not subside entirely, even by the time I packed my overseas bag and reluctantly left to return to a worse nightmare than Viet Nam, and that was to be a soldier turned civilian in the United States in September of 1968.

The radio was exploding with traffic, and the chaos and confusion of those first few hours was complete. Then Top got a handle on us, and little by little we got squared away and began to do our job. It was early afternoon on February 1st when we finally got to the house on Tu Do Street and found out what had happened. A squad of VC had broken in and demanded money and all the Americans there. They robbed

Mary's mother and executed every client they found, including the young Marine who had shot the Colonel. We had known she was forced to pay off the VC when they came to collect their taxes, and no one ever quibbled about it, for it had kept her operation safe, but this was a different story.

General Giap had masterminded the event that would eventually compel the French to leave Indo-China in 1954, and he was behind the Tet Offensive in 1968. There would be no going back to the way it was, and for a few days there in the first part of February, it was nip and tuck as to who would control Saigon. In the wild confusion, we were able to remove the American dead from the house on Tu Do Street and report them ambushed at various other parts of town.

Arty and I drew the task of removing the Colonel, and in our zeal to make his death look like it had happened somewhere else, we got ourselves into a tight spot down one of the million ill-lit side streets that would pass as a small, narrow alley. Only the presence of a VC captain we sometimes saw at the bar at the Tu Do Street house saved us. He stopped his men and asked us what we were doing in very passable English. There was no reason to lie to him, so we told him exactly what had happened.

"Sorry to be your enemy," he said, a weary sadness in his voice. "You go now. Don't come back here. There's no need you die."

We saluted him, and Arty backed the jeep straight back out of the alley at a speedy clip. When we were a bit closer to another American compound, we radioed in that we had found an ambushed American officer and requested an ambulance. We sat smoking over the machine gun mounted in the back of the jeep, keeping a wary eye out for anything moving. An eerie silence had fallen over the city, and the civilians stayed inside and off the streets. The only traffic had been our battalion, or the ARVN troops and QCs. There had also been elite VC units and NVA regulars. We watched the silvery shadows of the magnesium flares flickering about the darkened, silent streets, the quiet broken only by sporadic gunfire or the hissing static of the radio. We had turned it down to almost nothing, for there was no giveaway to your whereabouts quite like having a PRC-25 suddenly jolt into the noisy, quaint jabber of the battalion's business.

I can still see Arty's face in the liquid silver and black shadow, his hand cupping the cigarette to shield the glowing red eye. He was an innocent kid jaded by the huge black hole in the heart of the world that war always is, and it was mostly poetic justice that we spoke of then.

It is still mostly poetic justice that I speak of now, although I could never make sense out of his suicide, other than the fact that there are some things people may see that create wounds even deeper than any physical injury, that are so far-reaching they can never heal. Watching the last faint light flickering out on the desert skyline, I wondered about the murdered Colonel, and Arty, and the rest of my friends who died in that long ago war, passed and yet still passing, and about Mary and her mother, and where they got to and what happened to them. Maybe her mother should have sold her to the Colonel and let him bring her to America. It would have been Very Affordable Mary then.

As it was, sitting in the booth watching the dying storm, it seemed that the cost of it all was not countable in terms of money, or politics, or even morality-play lessons.

Top Shunk said that the things you remember in the stlllest part of night are the things you can hang onto. That might be something of an enigma, coming as it did from a professional soldier who had been in the service of his country through World War II, Korea, and Viet Nam. It also included long fishing stories, of streams in Colorado and Michigan, or rides in the back of a jeep passing by an ancient race of people pulling their handcarts full of rice to market, with that simple kindness that transcended even the war that raged about them.

I could thank Art and Top and all the rest for a lot of

memories like that, and they passed before me as I finished my meal and walked back to my room from the cafe.

Checking my bike, I could see the first, faint glimmer from the blanket of stars that were slowly beginning to twinkle, and there, right at the horizon directly to the east, out over the Bottomless Lakes, I saw a momentary brilliant flash of light that flared, then disappeared into the desert darkness.

Fearless Fred's

I can't remember hearing the round that killed him, but the look on the kid's face was one of total surprise, as if he had seen the bicycle under the tree on Christmas morning. He let out a little whisper of breath, and his eyes got very big, then he was gone, slumped over the sandbagged parapet the way a child lies down to take a nap. It was the first time I had seen someone I knew killed, and you're never the same again. There's a blackness that settles over your soul then, and no matter what you do to try to escape it, it's always there. You cross a line that you can never come back from once you start pulling triggers, and it follows you until the day you depart these plains of existence.

The training ground, it seems. Like some small kindergartens where we come back again and again, until we finally get our ticket out and go on to other things. That was apparent to me then, crouched in the dark next to the kid, and it was apparent to me sitting in a bar called Fearless Fred's years later. Fearless himself was going on about the disaster that had most recently befallen the Virgin Islands, and how the country as a whole was in trouble.

Fearless was a Marine in the Pacific during World War II and always wore a pistol when he held those kinds of discussions, to discourage any disagreements. On that particular day, Lew was on the day shift, and he was packing his own heat. He explained that it was to keep Fearless in line, and to keep tourists off cruise ships from ordering frozen rum drinks. It was a volatile group in those days, filled with the best of characters from all over the world. I lived next door to a basset hound named Beauregard, who was a terrible drunk and couldn't keep out of the Carousel Bar on the waterfront. His human mom was constantly on me for feeding him drinks. I protested that he was mean when he didn't get his scotch and milk, and it was bad for business to have a ninety-pound dog intimidating the customers, trying to get someone to stand him to a round or two.

Fearless liked to have Beauregard around, and he was fond of the fact that Mrs. Rabbit came in, as she was wont to do on her Wednesdays. That was the day she came to the main island to do her shopping and run her errands and visit with her friends at Secret Harbor. They had a bridge table there that even Fearless was afraid of approaching, for the old friends who played were of a steely-edged type who made Amarillo Slim look like a Sunday school choirboy and relentlessly cleaned out most newcomers. My grandfather could have sat in with them. He and his friends had invented a bridge-like game called Bear Tracks, so called because the fifth suit looked something like the track of a bear.

Five-suit bridge was something of an intimidating mystery then, and still is, although Mrs. Rabbit would have probably found it charming. She and her partner, Mr. Phillips, often sat with Fearless after one of their little games, counting their winnings and clucking their tongues at the language the proprietor sometimes used.

It was on one of those occasions that Mrs. Rabbit told me of the incident that had happened to her and her husband in China in 1937, after they had been interred by the Japanese invaders. I would have thought it was a harmless, interesting story told by an old woman who could skin the hide off you with her eyes if she chose, except for the fact of the UFO crash not a hundred miles from my old hometown. I began to believe the story was as literal a fact as one is ever liable to run into in this strange world getting stranger.

It had to do with an amulet that had come into Mrs. Rabbit's hand when she and Mr. Rabbit had first gone into the remote province where Walter had been hired to oversee a copper mine.

Mr. Rabbit was a large man and a well-known mining

engineer during those early years. He had come to the attention of an ancient cult known as the Tong, who kidnapped him and took him to a site where it looked like some sort of meteorite had hit. After he examined it further, it was evident an alien spacecraft had crashed.

He was forced to work on the site and managed to pick up some bit of the metal from the strange ship, for the impact had scattered smaller pieces that could be carried away.

Mrs. Rabbit showed me the amulet Walter had made her. She said it kept Mr. Rabbit alive. The Tong needed him to help them retrieve the secret of the crash. Her husband told her the leaders of the Chinese gang thought it was a piece of a puzzle that would unlock the door for them to overthrow the government and open the way for their organization to spread over the rest of the world. They already had footholds in the United States, where their members had gone long before as coolies to work in the vast, wide-open West. It was merely a matter of time, they thought.

The Japanese were of a more practical nature and wanted the captured mining engineer to help them extract more earthly ores. They took the larger samples he had on him when they marched in, but Mrs. Rabbit's amulet had been overlooked.

She told me the amulet was made of a metal her husband had never seen. Mr. Rabbit had been in the process of running tests and trying to unearth the ship when the Japanese invaded. The Tong moved the Rabbits to what they thought was a safe location in Manchuria, but the enemy soldiers were there before them. The Tong were killed or driven away, the Rabbits were moved, and Walter never had the chance to finish his work there, but it had puzzled him greatly over the years. The only proof he had that the craft ever existed was the amulet that Mrs. Rabbit kept hidden away. After the war, he sent it to a friend at Stanford for testing, but it aroused the curiosity of the staff, which made Mr. Rabbit nervous, and the amulet moved to its new home in the Virgin Islands still a mystery. They had brought an orphaned Chinese maid from one of the prison camps they had been in. She had seen the amulet once and said that it was a piece of the star that brought the Light Men.

She had originally been from Manchuria, where the UFO had come down. No one could say exactly when, the area was so removed from civilization, but the best records are often kept by the ones least trained in such matters, who refer to the extraordinary in the most ordinary of terms.

The Rabbits were moved all across those vast stretches of Manchuria, and Walter saw evidence of other sites that looked like the one he had found. He learned that the area known as the Bermuda Triangle is crisscrossed with possible underwater locations such as the ones he had seen years before in China. A French charter skipper who worked for the Water Isle Hotel, a regular at the Rabbits' house, had access to an electronics ship that plied the waters doing research for the oil companies. Maurice was looking for a sunken German U-boat that was unaccounted for, and so had the data on many miles of ocean floor between the continental United States and South American. There evidently was a lot to see for a man who knew of certain things to look for, even though they might be far below the surface of the sea.

The U-boat was found, along with three or four sunken sites that bore a resemblance to ancient ruins in Mexico and South America, sites some earlier explorers had referred to as ball courts, but which looked more like a NASA launching pad. The man who had walked on the moon said they had discovered something of a similar nature on the lunar surface, but it had not been a topic that was widely discussed behind the tight security of the space agency.

Walter Rabbit told his liberators from the Japanese internment camp of the strange wreckage he had seen in Manchuria, but they treated the report as though it was some trick his mind had played on him. They asked for the amulet to send away for tests, but Mrs. Rabbit had wisely "lost" it, and the

39

Rabbits never talked about it to officials for many years, until the French skipper showed up at the Water Isle Hotel.

Talking about those secrets with Mrs. Rabbit, I discovered there was something going on inside me, which had to do with that kid outside Tan Son Nhut, like where he'd gone, and what had happened, and why. That was Ernest Hemingway's code of writing: who was there, what happened, and how the weather was!

I remembered how the weather was the day that kid bought it, and who was there. I remember all the others, too. Mrs. Rabbit said she remembered those things, and that her husband had often talked just like that.

Even Fearless knew what I was talking about.

You'd never think a bar with a name like that would be a haven for spiritual seekers, but as it turned out, the place was full of people looking for the Road to the Sacred Mountain.

Whether they knew it or not.

Sometimes you found road signs in the strangest places, like the wilds of Manchuria, or the vast prairies near the Bottomless Lakes in New Mexico.

It was not lost on me that the first atomic bomb was tested not very far from the place near Roswell where the Sky Riders crashed.

That was as baffling as the look the kid had on his face at the end, as though he might have seen an alien walking up to the bunker. It was a look of wonder. I would have liked to ask him about what he was seeing, but there was no time.

My grandmother often had that sort of expression toward the last. She told me once, after I had been sitting in her den with her for quite some time, that she'd seen the Robert E. Lee, a stern-wheeler on the Mississippi, on its way up from New Madrid.

The further you go along, the more mysterious it gets.

If that's not a pip of a thing, I don't know what is.

Kind of like always having a fresh horse under you, no matter how close the posse gets.

The Man Who Walked on the Moon

I talked once with a man who had walked on the moon.

It was an ordinary conversation about an extraordinary event as we sat sipping our coffee in a front room in Beverly Hills, watching our hostess say goodnight to a guest. I never forgot the way he described how empty and alone he felt when they shut down the lunar lander on the surface of the moon. His big question was, will it fire back off again?

Just as they always describe a war as the Great War, if it's the war you've been in, I couldn't help noticing that the war I was caught up in seemed like a great war to me, especially in the midst of the sturm and drang of it, when the lead was flying so thick you could stand up and walk on it. Historically, the Great War was one of the ones I'd missed, not counting the fact that I indeed may have participated in another life. Not that I remember, but then again, what I've discovered is that all wars are pretty much the same, when you come right down to the nut-cutting. The calibers and millimeters may be different, but getting ventilated by a .303 Enfield or 7 mm. Mauser or Nambu or an AK-47 is all very well when you measure the size of the hole it puts through a hunk of flesh and bone. Being zapped by a rifle round or blown to smithereens by a laser-guided bomb doesn't meant doodly-squat in the long run.

Except that you've then been there and done that. Just like landing on the moon.

We awkwardly trundle off toward the stars like children learning to walk in a crib when we have the key to the doorway that would allow us to simply disappear and reappear there, without the hoopla, and certainly without the anxiety of "Will it start again?" to haunt us.

That's where we've found ourselves now, stuck somewhere

in this vast wilderness, having forgotten how to start it up and go back to where we belong.

That might be one of the reasons why we keep getting sucked into Great Wars, or dealing with plague, or natural disasters, because they are all reminders of how to restart the lander.

Odd thoughts, but given the inclination to go cosmic when faced with the very real possibility of being blown to Kingdom Come, it all seems in the perfectly natural order of things.

Stuck at a party in Beverly Hills is not quite the same thing as slinging lead on a hot, wet day outside the back gate of Tan Son Nhut, but it offered up its own dangers and pucker factors. Being there was a torment in its own right, like lying in the hooch looking at the beautiful round-eyed girls in Playboy magazine. Walking back to my car, counting the number of Mercedes-Benzes and Porsches and watching the people in the Old World cafe, I thought it all might be like training for a mission behind enemy lines, getting toughened up enough to take the punishment, no matter what they threw at you.

Like waiting in a pool of cold sweat inside that space suit, keeping your fingers crossed and rubbing your luck-piece, hoping that when you hit the button, the rocket engine beneath you would light off.

I've spent a good many days out of my life getting acquainted with that feeling, and on more than a few occasions I've felt my heart fall into my shoes when the button's pressed and nothing happens.

Like kicking over the Harley-Davidson in 1957 in front of the Dial Drive-In and almost being pitched head-first over the bars.

Norman Mailer wrote *The Naked And The Dead* after coming home from World War II, and many years later, he sat stranded in his Famous Suit, trying to remember what it was he'd had and where he'd put the keys to that sky chariot that would take him back to when he'd had it.

I have that cold chill down my back, like sitting in the wet darkness of the middle part of the night, listening to a small yellow man on the other side of the wall pull the pin out of the grenade and hearing the chemical fuse suddenly pop. Times like this make you wonder if the thing is going to come up, or will we all float on, drowning in this flood of lessons and distractions that keep us from looking straight at the smiling face of that big question.

When we hit the button, will it light off?

Or were we somehow mistaken? Are we on the right train?

When you reach here, where the body begins to rebel, and there isn't enough gas in the old lander, how will you get back to the Mother Ship?

Where is the road map to Old Dime Box? And why did they name it that? Does the little blue line on that state map draw on out into the Big Picture and signal an end to this life of a gypsy on the road forever?

Maybe Mrs. Rabbit knew about those things. I wish I'd asked.

The Hollow Earth Theory

I never thought much about the hollow earth theory until late August in 1968, on my way home to The World from Viet Nam. The stage then was a kaleidoscope of bizarre twists and turns and convoluted passages that began as wide open horizons, then swallowed in a gulp into dark, steamy tunnels that sucked the very breath from your lungs. It played like a light show, brilliant white and orange flashes with moments of shadow, electric and vivid against the mind's eye, etched forever, like the burn of "Willy Pete," or white phosphorus. My friend C.H. mentioned the hollow earth business on the way home from a run to Pinky's liquor store out on the Strip, and it hit me like a ton of bricks, or a concussion grenade, or the soft, warm pressure from a Saigon tea girl walking up and down your spine in a small room above Tu Do Street. It was so simple, it just was, and there was no further need to think about it or try to figure it out.

Adolph Hitler had gotten hold of it back when he was making a run for ruler of the world. The thing that interested him was that if the theory was correct, there would be oil reserves there, and he desperately needed oil to fuel his Blitzkrieg. Good old Adolph, always the one to be practical, even in the midst of the world on fire. I was a little more mystical in my pursuit of the idea, because in the back of my mind, there would be a little shelter there, and maybe a safe harbor to moor a nice little sailboat. Mrs. Rabbit, who was a landlady of mine shortly afterward, told me of her husband Walter's desire to have his sailboat tied up in his backyard, so they moved to the U. S. Virgins and bought a piece of land on Water Island, a small slip of land in the harbor of Charlotte Amalie, and he got his wish.

Mrs. Rabbit was always sad about the fact that Walter was

not still around, for she knew I would be all right if only he could have had a heart-to-heart talk with me.

I never knew how old she was, but she confessed to "about eighty," an age she wore wonderfully well. She must have been a striking beauty when she was Walter's young bride, away in a foreign land preparing to be devoured by the swelling tide of the Japanese emperor's armed might. She told me about China, where Walter was a mining engineer, and being held captive by the Japanese, who needed his expertise, sitting on her verandah overlooking Rabbit Point, with a view out toward Cat Island. Further on, when it was darker, you could see Puerto Rico twinkling in the night, like fallen stars in the vast, blue-black Caribbean.

She was fond of feeding the sea iguanas in the process of her morning swim. I would watch in amazement as the small dinosaurs took the lettuce leaves from her hand and slowly made their way back into the water to eat. They would never allow any other human to approach them on that small patch of beach that was her property, and people told me there were none of that species left in the waters surrounding the island. I thought of that in the same category as the idea that somewhere in the frozen Arctic there was a hidden cavern that would lead you down and down, into the hollow bosom of the earth, where there was another world, secret and inviolate, where the bewildered children of an angrier world could go for solace.

There was also an idea I had about the dolphins and Atlantis, which was not so far away from the other, and the sea iguanas served to strengthen it, converging as if in a great conference with Mrs. Rabbit on her morning swim.

Somewhere out in that great ocean, where the waters of all the world collide, their great salt body as one, it touched the white sand beach of Cam Ranh Bay in the South China Sea, and there must have still been echoes of another time, when the rock-'n'-roll music filled the air, and there was talk of short-timers and birds to The World. There was also the

Great Superstition Monster. which would bite if you did not have your luck-piece close to hand, or if you somehow tempted fate by daring to dream of landing unharmed back in Oakland or Fort Lewis. One wrong move, one careless slip, and it could mean you would end up like the ill-fated G.I. of a particular rumor that was rife for a long time, who was on the boarding ramp of his bird to freedom when a spent .50 caliber round took off the top of his head just as he reached out to touch the roundeyed stewardess who was welcoming him aboard.

We took those rumors to heart, and although it was never proven to be true, it was also never proven to be untrue. In matters of that nature that arise in a war, it was always more prudent to follow the advice of the wise Old Ones, who smeared buffalo grease on their shields to protect them from the White Eye bullets. Everything, your very life, depended on how strong your belief was that it would work.

The world was in a great flux then, and I sat on Mrs. Rabbit's verandah, one of the last sane places in the known universe, sipping Mount Gay rum and thinking about what it would be like going down that big cave leading to a secret road to the Inner World. Liberty boats from Marine landing craft and sailors from the nuclear carrier *Nimitz* showed up regularly, and Lew and Bobby One-Eye were always in brawls with the poor suckers, trapped on an island with plenty of cheap booze but no whores to keep them off the streets after they were too drunk to do anything but stir up trouble. I tried to explain all that to Mrs. Rabbit one night as we watched the harbor boil up with Shore Patrol and local police, trying to quell 2,500 drunken sailors off a giant aircraft carrier. It turned nasty later on, and the death of a local put the port offlimits for quite some time. Good for peace and quiet, but bad for the business we were in, which was tending bar, but Mrs. Rabbit was more blunt and to the point.

"Those boys should've been home with their families, not out loose without some good reason, or common sense. If

Walter were here, I'm sure he could have made them see the fact that what they were doing just wasn't right."

I agreed with her, as I always did, and respected Walter Rabbit as much as any man I never met. I expect he would have been a good man to cover your back in any sort of dustup, and I never doubted the size of his cojones, for I'd heard the story of how he'd won his last sailboat race at the ripe old age of ninety-two. Walter might have balked at being around Fearless Fred's when the night crew got rough, but then that wasn't what gentlemen escorting ladies did.

I'm sure if anyone had ever slighted his lady, there would have been an old-fashioned, Victorian hell to pay.

Mrs. Rabbit was full of surprises, as we found out not too much later, when she was jumped by a pair of muggers outside Trader Dan's on the waterfront, where she had gone by cab to meet with a realtor about some property she had put up for sale. The word was out almost instantly, but before Bobby One-Eye, or Lew, or any of the rest of our Main Street Mob could arrive to save her, she had rescued herself by pulling a snub-nosed .38 out of her purse and firing off a warning shot that startled the donkeys and roosters into a wild, raucous opera that went on half the night.

A .38 S&W in Mrs. Rabbit's purse lent weight to the whole idea of there being a secret, sacred road to salvation, whether it be with Paul and the Burning Bush on the road to Damascus, or a cavern beneath the Arctic leading to a safe haven that was exactly like the back verandah of Mrs. Rabbit. It even came with small yellow and black birds, the bananaquit, who were made famous in the calypso song "Yellow Bird."

Bobby One-Eye wasn't so sure about the Hollow Earth theory, but he never ceased to be amazed at the crazy twists life took, or the bent existence of the citizens of the islands. Mrs. Rabbit was one of those ironies which rendered you helpless in the light of the fact that she was somehow in charge of rounding up what was left of the boys who'd gone bad, just

47

as Walter would have liked her to do, and if you came to her attention, you could pretty well count on being squared away before she made her yearly pilgrimage back to Seattle, where she did, as she put it, penance for being old but still able to drive. Her three elderly sisters lived there and waited all year for her to come home to drive them all off on one of their trips.

She mentioned the Hollow Earth business to her sisters one summer, and they eagerly decided it would be a vastly desirable cruise to take, and began searching about for information. I waved good-bye to her from the deck of the Water Island ferry and watched her cab leave the dock. Her sparkling blue eyes were as fierce as a hawk's that day, and she regaled me with instructions.

I was too preoccupied with another matter at the time, and it was not until a month later that I got word that she was going to rent out Rabbit Point to a resort hotel, and did not plan to come back to St. Thomas. It was what she had been trying to point out to me all along, when she was giving me detailed instructions regarding feeding the sea iguanas, and what mixture of sugar and water to mix for the yellow and black birds.

"All that business about there being somewhere under the earth is just poppyrot," she confided as she got out of the jeep at the ferry dock. "If I were you, I'd take a look at where you are, and know that's exactly where you need to be."

Mrs. Gertrude Rabbit, age somewhere around eighty, feeding the sea iguanas on the small sandy beach at Rabbit Point, looking out at the sea her Walter sailed on until he finally made that last passage, one that took him to the foot of the trail of the real Journey, where we're all bound.

Little Mouse in the Ferrari

Whoever thought the road to the Sacred Mountain would run such a twisted, convoluted course?

Would it have occurred to anyone that Little Mouse would disappear in Nick's Ferrari, or that Nick would die of AIDS, and Gordon would be dead on a chaise lounge in a tux for his own wake, while the video he'd made weeks before played to the gathering?

I never would have thought for a moment I'd be caught up in the midst of the Radical Faeries during the Human Rights March on Washington in April of that year, when but a few months before I had been there as a Vietnam Vet, at the gathering of the clan before the Wall.

Mrs. Rabbit tried to warn me about all this on more than one occasion, sitting at her table on the verandah overlooking the small beach below the Water Isle Hotel, having tea with a man who knew all there was to know about hydroponic gardening.

But I digress and shoot forward a bit, curling over into the clouds, like the World War II movies of fighters coming out of the sun, guns blazing. There is some of that in this yarn too, because as I write this, it is almost sixty years since they loaded up every boat and ship and plane they could round up, and set off on a great quest across the English Channel, to storm the gates of Fortress Europe. If you were only born lately, it won't carry much weight, and you won't have a twinge in that part of you that records all great things, to bring it back later, where it will play in your head like an old movie classic all night long.

I was three years old, but I remember sitting in my grandmother's lap while she and my grandfather listened to the news of D-Day on the radio. They had two sons in the war, and even as a child that small, I felt their anxiety and concern. I did my part for the war effort on a train ride to Las Vegas a short time afterward, when we went to visit my grandmother's sister. The train was full of troops, and from somewhere I had learned that old soldier's ditty, "Praise the Lord and Pass the Ammunition." My grandmother told me that story years later, and said the soldiers passed me from one to another up and down the car, laughing and making a fuss over me. I wish I had memories of that, but it is one of those strange mental blanks you get at times. I do have memories of riding on my cousin Byron's Indian in Las Vegas, and my grandmother being terrified that I was on a motorcycle. Maybe that's where I went wrong, riding on my cousin Byron's Indian in Las Vegas in 1944.

It's a good thing to have in your memory bank, even if you can't recall singing that great old song, "Praise the Lord and Pass the Ammunition." That may have been the exact moment that I knew my ride for the trip to the Sacred Mountain would be aboard a motorcycle. They didn't make the Indian Chief for many years, but it was enough to make a lasting impression on my young mind. I'm sure there were other things that registered on me in those days, but none could compete with the big red Indian Chief.

The photos in my grandmother's albums are in black and white, but I know the Chief is red, and that my cousin Byron was a handsome young man. Byron Underhill. With his looks and a name like that, he should have been in movies and hung out in Hollywood, but he didn't. My cousin Tommy was handsome too, and rode a motorcycle as well, but Lake Mead got him. He traded in his yen for motorcycles and bought big, fast powerboats, but he should have stayed with the Indians.

At least they wouldn't drown you.

My Uncle Robert went back to France fifty years after he went the first time, in June of 1944. It took a long time to grasp the moment of that. I have watched the years roll by since I

50

came home from Viet Nam in the late summer of 1968, and am only now far enough distanced to begin to understand the necessity of returning.

I stood next to a small, white-haired lady in an exhibit room at the Holocaust Memorial in Washington on the day before it was open to the public and felt time reverse itself. The difficult thing about being in those places is that you can't just look at a static display. You are standing next to a survivor of one of the camps that are in the memorial, and you are not given the luxury of emotional distance. I have experienced that at the memorial where the names of my fallen comrades are chiseled into the black stone, and at a showing of the AIDS Quilt at the foot of the Washington Monument. Three very separate events, but all the very same loss and sorrow, and a stronger sense of celebration of life, and of those who have survived to bear testimony and share the strength and hope that is born of that total black despair and horror.

My wife's brother Nick was as handsome as my cousin Byron, but he was gay. He didn't ride Indian Chiefs, he was a cinematographer, and he filmed the 85th Harley-Davidson Anniversary Ride to Milwaukee. I enjoyed his humor and grew to a new understanding of courage under fire. It was different than what I experienced as a young soldier in Indo-China, but it was of the same source. Looking backwards from our place in the Cosmic Circus Parade, it falls out in every generation that there is a Great Test by Fire. Events so overwhelming that the world is thrown into the maelstrom, and every single person alive is caught up in it.

No one ever said the Road to the Sacred Mountain would be so difficult, or so hard to find. It took the incident of Little Mouse taking Nick's Ferrari to point out another side of the whole affair.

Little Mouse went with my wife to stay with Nick when he was dying of AIDS. He found a home in a small scale model of that same Ferrari Testarossa that I saw in Roswell,

New Mexico, in 1957. After Nick's death my wife searched the house for Little Mouse, but he and the car were gone. The car has since shown back up, packed and sent to her by a friend of her brother's, but there has been no word of Little Mouse, although I have no doubt that he has arrived at his destination. When you embark onto troubled seas, the departure does not matter so much as the arrival, whether you're in a Ferrari, or on an Indian Chief, or in Charlie Norton's case, aboard a cow pony named Star.

The confusing thing is, there was no instruction book when we started out on this wild and winding trail. I thought my friend Delbert Lingneau might have been right all those years ago, just taking a wife, and wanting to raise wheat and cotton and go into town on Saturday nights for ice-cream. The Dial Drive-In was the repository of many childhood hopes and fantasies, but I would bet there was not one back then that had anything to do with finding a clear road sign to the Sacred Mountain. Mine had something to do with a 1957 Porsche Speedster, and being able to mumble like James Dean did in "Rebel Without a Cause".

His steed was a 1955 Porsche Spyder, and he crashed it on Highway 46 in Central California, on the way to a road race. I have been by the spot since and stopped at the small cafe in Cholame, where a Japanese fan has made a memorial to James Dean from steel and wood. It's an eerie spot for one who was alive when Dean was. Riding in on my bike, I could imagine that low-slung German racing car hurtling down that rural road, and almost feel the impact as the farmer pulled onto the highway to go into Cholame for coffee with his friends. Dean's mechanic, a German who was riding with him, survived, only to be killed years later in an accident on an autobahn in Germany. Those circles are closed now, but you can still feel traces of them when you're out nosing around for clues.

I stop in Cholame for coffee at that cafe, and ride Highway 46 on down to the coast, and go up to Willy Hearst's joint,

San Simeon. His nickname was Billy Buster, and his mom sounded like a neat lady. She'd throw parties for him in the summer and have a circus tent put up, and he could invite all his friends from San Francisco up for camp. When he grew up, he built San Simeon and did the same. I liked him, because he had secret passages built into the place so he could make great entrances, and he loved beautiful things. It helped that he had a ton of money. He would be an example to follow if I ever hit the lottery, or had a runaway bestseller.

If you want to find out a person's true nature, give them a lot of money. Old Chinese were fond of saying that.

And if you want to kill a man, heap praise on him.

A Brother and His Hostage

It was sometime in 1983 that I first heard the story about what had happened to Tennessee Williams. I must have read it in the paper or seen it on the TV, but it didn't hit home until I'd had a chance to mull it over, like a bear who has holed up in his cave for the winter. I ended up doing a book about it, but it's still on my mind, just like the war, or the Sky Riders' crash in 1947.

There's a big billboard outside Deming, New Mexico, that reads, "Home of pure water and fast ducks!" Maybe they've put one of those up on the way to St. Louis, reading, "Tennessee Williams, prisoner of death! See him at the XYZ Cemetery and Mausoleum!"

Like having your gizzard blown out by an AK-47 round, or stepping on a Bouncing Betty, it has a way of getting your attention. Only this was subtle, the way things usually get when the big boys don't want you to know too much about they they're up to. Mainly because they don't know themselves, but they couldn't very well be acting the way they do unless they have some sort of code or secret, which they hold out as the reason why they're doing anything.

Tennessee's brother's reasons might well sum up all the reasons, whether it be a justification for going to war, or to the moon, or just not telling you why you have to pay income tax, and that's simply that he was mad at his brother for being famous, and he wasn't. And they were brothers, which means the playing out of the worst sort of karma one could imagine.

Every time I go to New Orleans, I can't help watching for Blanche and Stanley. They were characters out of one of his famous plays. And the streetcar named Desire sits there in that steamy city, waiting and waiting, just like Tennessee in that dark vault in St. Louis, dreaming of the Gulf Stream and those cool, shark-eyed depths off Cuba where Hart Crane went over the stern of the ship.

That's where Tennessee wanted to be. But he's ended up in St. Louis.

I spent a long time in the islands of the Caribbean. Every night I would look out over my verandah toward Puerto Rico and Miami and think of those tremendous ocean mountains beneath me, and wonder how long it would take for a body to reach the bottom of the trench out there. My wife is terrified of a watery death, but they have said that once you're past the panic of not being able to breathe, it is very peaceful, like returning to the womb. A psychic in Virginia Beach told me that she saw me as a young black man standing in a boat, watching a huge tidal wave coming toward me, and that I had a beautiful smile on my face, with no fear at all. This was in the city of the Edgar Cayce Institute, the Association for Research and Enlightenment, A.R.E. They have a wonderful old library there, with a reading room overlooking the Atlantic. I always believed Edgar was right when he said Virginia Beach was one of the mirror cities, which meant that a city in our plane of existence mirrored a twin city just above it, on the next level up. I think that goes for people, too. The Higher Self, if you will.

The place is full of studies like that. Along with the largest naval installation in the United States, which gives it a very eclectic sort of feel. Horny sailors mixing with soul travelers and students of the occult, all thrown into a space that harks all the way back to the lost colony at Roanoke, which always struck my fancy. No one has anything but theories about where they went, but I've always kind of held with the idea that the spirit guides out of Atlantis came and saved them from starving to death that first winter they were left there. Sitting on that verandah in the islands, I thought a lot about where Atlantis might be, and it came to me one night as I watched the lights in the harbor of Charlotte Amalie that I was perched on one of the mountaintops of that fabled land. My house would have been at an altitude of about 24,000 feet, if all the water were drained out of the Caribbean, Atlantic, and Gulf of Mexico, and you could walk from Miami to St. Thomas.

About the time the UFO was crashing out in New Mexico, my grandfather took my grandmother and me to St. Louis to see the zoo there and to see the St. Louis Cardinals play. That was a trip, sitting out in the stands, chomping on the hot dog and wearing my new, real wool, authentic St. Louis Cardinals hat. I saw Ted Williams play. I don't remember if my team won or not, but I remember the ride back to the hotel in the car. We drove very slowly down toward a place my grandmother remembered as a child, a place with a wonderful name, Creve Coeur. I looked out the back window with a kid's sleep eyes and wondered at a city with so many streetlights, and a ballpark, and a zoo.

That was still a time of wonder, before all the rest of the rehearsal started. I had been to St. Louis, and seen monkeys riding bicycles, and Ted Williams hit a home run, and Old Man River himself. And I got to go back the next year, when my grandfather and grandmother took me after his mother's funeral up in the Ozarks. On that trip, I saw Uncle Ben, who was actually my grandmother's sister's husband, who had lost his fingers in sawmill accidents, and his dog, Zip, who played with me out under the trees while they buried the handmade pine box. On the way back down the red clay road, the car got stuck, and a man with two mules came and pulled us free. For the first time ever, I saw my grandmother really frightened, although I couldn't see what had scared her about sliding off in a ditch and getting stuck. Even as a kid, I picked up on that terror she was feeling, much like what Tennessee must have felt when he knew they were putting him into that mausoleum.

I never understood that fear until years later, when I heard the full story. My grandparents had been moving to New Mexico in an open-top touring car in 1925, and just outside Alamogordo, where they tested the first atom bomb, they crashed. It was after dark, and my mother's baby sister was trapped under the wreckage. My grandfather had to walk to find help, leaving his wife and three small children there alone in the dark. The little sister died there. My uncle and my mother and their mother huddled alone there in the dark, with the little dead girl trapped under the car, until my grandfather came back with a man who had a team of mules.

Knowing what I know now, I guess when my grandmother saw the man with the mules, she had a flashback to her birthday in 1925, when her little baby daughter was killed. My grandfather kept patting my grandmother on the arm, soothing her as he would a child, while the man pulled us out. I sat in the backseat of the big gray Chrysler, watching the two animals strain and tug, and knew there was a big world full of sometimes odd surprises in store.

When we got home, I had nightmares about seeing the dried-up old woman in the rough pine box. I dreamed she was reaching up to grab me, and wouldn't let me go, even when they began to pile the cold earth on top of us. Zip was there barking, but I couldn't get away until the man with the mules appeared and put me on top of one of the animals. We walked away down a red clay road through a lot of trees. Then there were chimpanzees on bicycles, chattering and baring their teeth, until I woke up in the dark room, calling out for my grandfather. He would come and talk to me, and look under the bed to make sure there was nothing there, and leave a light on, so I could see there were no alligators under the bed.

I was thinking about Tennessee the last time I sat by the Mississippi. I was talking to Ned Virgin and watching that river roll slowly by me, with the great ocean-going vessels that were moored on its broad back. I wished I could have gone back and found a man with a team of mules to pull down that prison where he's trapped. I thought about that a while, wondering where he'd go and who he'd see there. There was a man with a horn playing on the sidewalk behind me, joined by a man on a standup bass. I heard the music and felt the city and watched a freighter sliding down the back of the brown river, slipping silently on out into the Gulf Stream further down, past Pilot Point. I could close my eyes and imagine my grandmother, when she was young and very beautiful, sitting in a lace dress with a big hat, singing one of the river songs her father had taught her, watching the days and months slip by, blending in with the river, back where she began, and Tennessee, a peaceful look on his face, not unlike that on Ned Virgin's, hearing the song of the open sea, and freedom.

You may ask, have we ever gone to get Tennessee, my friends and I?

I wonder. I've gone in my dreams, and in my book about it, but I think of Edgar Cayce's mirror-universe theory, and it seems more than possible that we have already freed Tennessee, although he certainly cannot be thought of as anything other than free, having already slipped these bonds of earth and exited to the Green Room.

It may be something entirely different. My old friend Barry Braden had an uncle who believed he had been killed in World War I, and that this existence he was living was nothing but the worst parts of hell. When I think of that, it's not so far removed from the truth, on any given day.

Except that there's this unreasonable seed of hope that was planted somewhere back in the past, and no matter how dark or brutal it looks, there's this sliver of eternal optimism that it's all going to work out all right.

The river runs too close there in St. Louis, and the call would be too great to resist. It never forgets, just like the sea or a war. They keep their dead in a very sacred trust, unlike other more transient things.

Someone might have to go check out Tennessee's mausoleum in St. Louis one of these days. It may not come as too big a surprise to find an empty casket.

The Best Tenor in the Crow's Nest

His name was Johnny, and he had the sort of skull you saw in the pictures of Papa Doc's Tontons Macoutes, a slight sloping of the forehead, and a thick neck to hold it. He began showing up at the Crow's Nest when we had the round-robin singalongs and poetry happenings. When he opened his mouth, the sweetest tenor voice we'd ever heard came out. His favorite song was "Where Have All the Flowers Gone?" It was the eeriest thing, this pure, sweet voice coming from such a menacing man. But he liked Scott, so there was never any trouble when he came to sing.

Janis Joplin showed up one night at the Crow's Nest and sang along with Johnny for a while. I wrote her a poem on one of the roof beams, and she gave me a peck on the cheek. That was something, getting a peck on the cheek from Janis Joplin. We went to the Crazy Cow for something to eat and walked up Back Street to Danny Unkey's Sand Box. She had brought a guitar picker from John Lee Hooker's bunch down with her, to try to put together a new band of her own. I liked the guy, who was from Nashville. He had a thing for Mount Gay rum, so we became fast friends, and it was fun to listen to him and Scott run names by each other, which would read like a who's who of famous musicians.

There was a Van Morrison imitator from Puerto Rico playing the club that night, but he was sent back to his hotel early, and my friend Scott and the drummer out of the Beach Boys sat in with Joplin and her axe man, and I was treated to one of those occasional bits of life that is more starkly real than reality. More haunting, as well. I sat at the bar in Danny's joint full of bottled sunshine, listening to Joplin and Scott sing a song he'd recorded earlier, called "Reason to Believe."

They did it a cappella, and the place was silent. Even the drunks knew they were listening to something they would never likely hear again. After they finished and turned to a louder, more hard-rocking tune, it was apparent to all that something had happened, some cosmic curtain had parted for just the faintest of moments, and sounds from the rehearsal halls in the Big Room drifted out onto the late-night crowd.

I had heard the classical guitarist Segovia play once in the town he was named after. There were forty chairs in a hallway of a church, which was said to have perfect acoustics, and we sat waiting for the master. He was old then, and looked barely able to cross the floor to get to his stool, but the moment he had his guitar in his hands, he was transformed. We sat while he played a stunning program for over an hour. There was no applause, merely listening in silence. l have wondered at odd times what it would feel like to just walk into God's office and sit down for a chat. That night in Segovia was close to it, and years later, listening to Janis Joplin and my friend Scott was another.

I had experienced it more than once in the war, when the air was so full of lead you could have walked on it, and everything became perfectly still. You could hear your blood in your ears, and every single molecule in every single thing seemed to be straining to be let out. The sunlight was something out of Van Gogh, and a cigarette tasted like the very best thing I had ever had. Seconds were precious, and my life at that single passing instant, passed and passing, was the Alpha and the Omega, all that was, and all that mattered.

I was aware that death was with us at Danny's club. It was like another sense that developed in the war. Some said you learned to smell death on someone. It's not an actual sense, but it's just as real, and it was very strong in the Sand Box that night. I was full of Mount Gay rum, but I still felt it, and I tried to dismiss it. Hearing that Joplin was gone a few months later, it made the evening that much more etched into my memory. If I get very quiet sometimes, I can still hear Scott and Janis singing that song, that haunting refrain just as clear now as it was in that early-morning hour in my friend's club.

I had arrived late to the dance, but I was suddenly in the midst of everything. There was a steady flow of names and faces drifting through Charlotte Amalie then. John Phillips and the Mamas and Papas started the run on St. Thomas when they hung out in the islands before going back to the States to record "California Dreamin'."

It was where I met Pittsburgh, better known as Mr. Pitts, a steel-gray cat the same color as the city, who is plaguing me still with his long-distance calls from all over the world, and Scott McKenzie, who was in the islands trying to get his act back together after having to deal with mega doses of fame from his music.

I first heard McKenzie's song "San Francisco" in July of 1967, when I was at the Oakland Army Replacement Depot, getting ready to ship out for Okinawa and on to Viet Nam. There were pictures of beautiful flower children on the tube, and free love was a rumor, but I was located across the Bay from it all, getting ready to go off to a war. I had used the last two days of my leave to stay at the Mark Hopkins Hotel in San Francisco, but I never got out of the bar downstairs. Jack Daniels took the place of a beautiful hippie lady to send me away, and I had no pleasant memories of that Summer of Love that was taking place there.

The next thing I knew, the man who had sung it was using my room in the small hotel in St. Thomas to try to lay the waitress I'd had a crush on since I arrived in the islands. Our relationship was always like that, and still is. Love/hate. He had a twelve-string Guild guitar that knew wonderful songs, and when we had those singalongs at the Crow's Nest, time stood still for a while, and all that was wrong with the world was made right.

It seemed so easy. There was an innocence then that I still believe in, a belief that something could be done, and would be done, there seemed to be so many young people willing to do it. There were drugs, to be sure, but they were nothing more than an identity, a symbol of the clan, a hospitable offering to any stranger who might happen across your campfire.

Johnny brought along his bodyguard, a small, older man, which seemed strange until he pulled back his sport coat and displayed his impressive array of hardware.

Another old Chinese adage that had floated around forever. Never let anyone see your true strength. Shadow and light, just like the war, ghost-like figures flitting in and out of the shimmering magnesium flarelight.

Were they real or imagined?

Like Janis Joplin and Scott singing "Reason to Believe" that late evening in 1969. There was talk of going to Woodstock, but Scott wouldn't go. He was having trouble picking up the Guild. We couldn't tell if it was writer's block, or if he was having a bout of guilty conscience for using his great talent and charisma to lure the next sweet young thing into his web.

Johnny came every night to watch us write poetry on the roof posts, and there was the other surrealistic event of that summer of 1969, the landing on the moon.

I sat in that same bar, leaning out to look up at the full moon above the Caribbean, then back to the black-and-white TV that was on the bar, watching Neal Armstrong set foot on the lunar surface. I was full of rum as usual, but great moments reach through alcohol or drug fogs to touch that very innermost part of us which is the receptor to the road signs Home. Johnny was there that night too, and I began to enjoy a large dose of displaced celebrity, for the man who had touched down first on the moon carried my first name. Johnny couldn't seem to get enough of shouting out my name gleefully and clapping me heartily on the back. It made no difference that I spelled my name Niel. Or rather my mother did, her way of setting me apart from my peers. No branch of government has ever spelled it the way she did without a fight. Everyone from the DMV to the United States Army insisted on correcting it. Neal, or Neil, or Kneel has followed always. It's spelled Niels in the Scandinavian countries, but no one in the United States will accept that easily. It has been a battle all my life to convince any clerk or secretary anywhere that it is indeed spelled the way it is.

The good thing is, you never for a moment forget who you are.

When I met and talked to the man who had walked on the moon years later, it wasn't the one with my name.

It would have been a circle closing if it had been the other way, but what I have seen of circles is that you never know where you're going to end or begin.

Johnny the crime-boss with the very small bodyguard went on singing "Where Have All the Flowers Gone?," and Joplin was gone.

Scott drifts in and out of my life as shadow-like as one of my old enemies in Viet Nam. You go to the moon and still end up standing around a cocktail party in Beverly Hills, or survive a war, yet the war never leaves.

The Five-Sided Chinese Mirror.

Whether it's a punishment or blessing depends on how you view the reflection.

Dances from Argentina

She smelled of the tropical mystery of the Pampas and spoke English with a lilting rhythm of the wild music from her home.

Everyone I knew was hopelessly in love with her in 1966, but her heart belonged to a Brazilian guitarist named Luis.

It was a difficult summer.

There was Maria, so desirable, yet unattainable, and then there was the draft, lurking around every campus like a shadow of the black plague, although the death count would not be known for another seven years or more. Volatile times, as my old friend Mole would say, off to another meeting of one radical group or another.

As often happens when you are in the midst of something that big, you only get brief glimpses of it, like the lookout on the Titanic that fateful night in 1912, just a small, slightly shimmering tower of ice that looked so beautiful in the dark water.

We drank and stayed up every day until dawn, wrote poetry, sang songs, and did madcap, romantic things, like stealing roses for our girls from the city nature gardens. Champagne and brandy flowed, and day by day we were bombarded with the Beatles and the war that was beginning to rage in Southeast Asia, along with the usual concerns of university students, grades and our deferments.

One by one, our numbers dwindled, and the parties grew fewer and further between as the crowd was scattered to the winds that blew helter-skelter across the world, separating friends and families, tumbleweeds drifting out across the wilderness of the plains, on and on, until in time it was difficult to even find someone to talk long distance to.

Mike Myrick could still puke a horizontal spout that held the record forever, but Mickey Byrd vanished into the Nebraska outback just as slickly as he had vanished that night on Reese AFB, which brought out the Air Police, causing such a stir that we were unceremoniously banned from ever going there again. And Mickey had managed to completely ruin a perfectly good sport coat I had lent him so they would let him into the Officers' Club.

Reese AFB, as I have since noticed, is on a grid that intersects the UFO crash in Roswell, but I didn't pay much attention to that knowledge at the time. There was the old Leftwich Legend as well, but I wasn't able to piece the mystery of it all together until much later. The trail was as cold as the blue northers that used to blow across these prairies. There were people who seemed to know some part of the secret, but they were being disappeared left and right. Anyone who had any knowledge of the Road to the Sacred Mountain was extremely dangerous to those in power.

In those days, it was easy to discredit anyone with a simple twist of a phrase. "He's a drunk. He's a drugger. Look at him. Seeing little leprechauns crawling out of the light switch, no doubt."

I wasn't alone in not quite being able to grasp all the pieces and parts of the puzzle that began to pile up as evidence of the existence of the Road, and that there was more afoot than I thought.

Or than anyone thought.

Mrs. Leftwich was the widow of a rancher in the part of the country I grew up in, so old and withered that her bones seemed to rattle in the West Texas winds that are always blowing. She would come to my grandmother's house when I was small and sit on the edge of her chair with her silver ear-trumpet clutched in her birdlike hand. My grandmother would pour her another cup of tea and ask her about the Judge, who had been dead for more than forty years.

I was always terrified of Mrs. Leftwich. The veins in her hands and face ran so close to the surface they looked like tangled blue spider webs, and her eyes were as piercing as a hawk's.

She spoke of many things the judge did and said, but I was too afraid of her to notice until I got older. Then I would hide in the room next to where my grandmother and Mrs. Leftwich were visiting and listen to them talk. She always started with the same sinister story, about how the Judge was set on by thieves in the night. He had chased them away, but that was what brought on the fits, and eventually his death. When she told about the fits, she contorted her face into a hideous mask that made me hide my eyes and sent me scampering away into the safety of my grandmother's kitchen.

In my child's imagination, I began to fabricate a great treasure hidden in the old ranch house at the edge of my small town, its roof drooping, its windmill blades snaggled like a beggar's teeth. Running in a lop-sided fashion, that windmill made eerie, screeching noises in the night when she had forgotten to lock it, and on more than one occasion I would be riding my bicycle out near the old homestead and fly away, my heart thundering in my mouth, sure I was hearing the ravings of the old Judge, out to catch any thief that might be coming for his hidden treasure.

I also heard stories from Mrs. Leftwich of a great White Buffalo that came onto the Judge's ranch just before he died. It was nothing but a scary old woman's story then. I didn't realize that I was hearing a plain report of the Road, and didn't come to understand the importance of her tale until after I came home from the war.

Sometimes you carry a piece of information for years, not knowing what it is. Like having a key for a lock you haven't found yet, or a map of a country you have never heard of.

It does not make that key or that country invalid.

I found out more about the old woman and her husband

from Calvin Blaine, a blacksmith. He and his friends were older than I was when Mrs. Leftwich was still alive, and they played some cruel teenage pranks on her until the sheriff put a stop to it. In another year, three of the friends had joined the army and were on their way to the Korean War. They had a last big blast at the now deserted old place, and someone got the idea of starting a fire to keep warm. It caught the floor afire, and in short order the ancient house was gone, taking with it any hopes I ever had of finding that elusive treasure of the old mad Judge.

Calvin told me it was where they would go park with their girlfriends back when the old woman was still alive. She was almost totally deaf and didn't hear the hot-rod Fords or Chevys pulling behind her stock tank so the kids could make out in the back seat. He was there one night in early January with his sweetheart and had left the motor running to keep them warm. Looking up at the instrument panel to check that the motor wasn't overheating, he saw the outline of some sort of large white animal standing on its hind legs not five feet from his car.

He jumped up so quickly he hit his head on the roof and scared his girl so badly that she screamed, thinking she'd been caught by her father. Calvin crawled into the driver's seat and gunned the car out of the rough dirt road behind the windmill, not stopping until he hit the paved county highway a half-mile away. His girl was sure it was just light reflecting off the snow and got so angry with him for scaring her that she never would park there to make out again.

He told me he went back to the spot after he'd taken her home and parked behind the stock tank to get out and take a look around.

In the glare of the headlights on the snow, he was sure he'd seen distinct hoof prints in the area where he thought the large white animal had been. Everyone he told that to insisted it must have been cows back there, although Mrs. Leftwich didn't have livestock anymore, and there were no cattle within five miles of the place.

Calvin always thought the thing he had seen was a White Buffalo, and that it was some sort of warning to him, because he saw it again in Korea. It came on a night when they had been overrun by the enemy and he had been left for dead in the snow. He was on the point of giving up and calling out, hoping that someone would come and shoot him. Instead he opened his eyes and looked directly up into the kind, unblinking glance of some sort of giant being, all white.

"Looking back on it," he said, "I remember reading about the Indians and their buffalo. That's what it was. Only huge and white."

Calvin had been fond of whiskey ever since he and one remaining classmate had come home from the Army, but I didn't attribute the story of the White Buffalo to Jack Daniels. Calvin was a wild one, but not the sort to let his imagination get away from him. He ended up marrying the girl who had been parked with him that night behind the stock tank at Mrs. Leftwich's place and settled down into a routine of life that must have been very trying. The girl grew into a woman, and had his son and daughter, then left him.

He was dead in a drunken car wreck a year or so later. It had been a cold February night, with a light dusting of snow on the ground. The Highway Patrolman who'd investigated said it looked as though he'd swerved to miss something in the road.

Nobody ever said what, but I always felt that if I'd gone there that night, there would have been hoof prints across that part of the highway.

Not of cattle, but of a great white being that came out of nowhere, and went back again.

You can watch for them in that part of the country in the colder part of the year. Mooch Crane claimed the icy weather made his bones ache so much he couldn't play dominos at Rusty's. He had also heard of the rumor about the White Buffalo. He was a practical man in most respects, but trying to search out a great white being was too tempting a thing to overlook.

Mooch managed to get his wife settled into a new house his oil money had paid for, and she carpeted it all in a soft white. To avoid nasty things happening to her beautiful white floors, she built an exact replica of her house, only smaller, so her husband could wash up and change shoes before he came in. He did that without fail for years until they found him early one morning, sitting in his pickup out on one of the turn rows on his spread. The motor was running, and he was smiling, as though remembering something he'd forgotten long ago, or maybe it was what I've always suspected, that he'd finally seen the White Buffalo, and it had come to take him home.

It was quite a thrill, coming along over those vast, wide open plains and seeing a homestead in the distance. Even when I was growing up, it had an impact as you neared a place, and you would slowly watch it grow up from the very earth. Mooch always loved the effect his wife's little joke had on people, and he would be horribly disappointed to know that whoever bought the house after they retired from this mortal coil moved their German shepherd into the old Small House, as Mrs. Crane called it, and advertised a very good buffet ready to be put out for guests at the bed and breakfast, which catered to clients from the "city" who came for the pheasant hunting, an event that had become big in later years. You would have to have reservations a year in advance to get in on one of the hunts now. Someone saw that was good business, and started stocking more birds, and leasing more land to run them on.

Marla had seen that Small House and the odd phenomenon of the optical illusion it gave to anyone traveling along the highway.

You'd look off into the near distance, and there would be these two houses, exactly alike. It made you think your eyes were gone haywire. I talked Maria into riding down with me from college to look at the sights and get away from the turmoil of trying to do her thesis. I thought it might avail me an opportunity to make points with her, but all she talked about was Luis and when they were planning to go to New York, where he could pursue his music. The other downer was that she hated Mike Myrick, because he had ruined a carpet in her rental apartment with one of his longer-than-a-hose horizontal pukes, and I had been the one who had invited him.

There was nothing to do in the small town, and I used it for a drying-out time to try to recover from the brutal pace I had been used to. That was the year my mother got the classic 1966 Buick Riviera Gran Sport, black on black. It was also the year I was called up for a pre-induction physical. The odd thing was, I was relieved to get it. Everyone else was dreading the day the doom message would be delivered, but the day mine came, I felt a lightness of being that I had not felt since I was a small child riding in the front part of the saddle on my cousin Byron's Indian.

About that same time, there was a skeleton discovered in the well on the old Leftwich place, found by a survey crew who were making the site ready for the new house and barn that was to be put there. The remains were determined to be those of a male approximately fifteen years of age, but there was no identification ever made, and in the end, the sheriff had "it" buried in a field behind the local cemetery. There is a marker there to this day, inscribed with the saddest of words, "Unknown."

Maria had been raised in a household in Argentina that believed in the old-fashioned ways. She was known for her psychic visions, and we went to the cemetery and sat with a picnic lunch out among the tombstones, most of them with names I had grown up with, with faces attached and memories that went a long way back. She sat on the grave of the mysterious person who had ended up in the well on the old Leftwich place, playing with a blade of grass and looking out over the vast prairie that sloped ever so slightly away to the Gulf of Mexico, covered in a rich patchwork blanket of corn and wheat and cotton. The smell of the afternoon was late September, and I watched her move, her dark eyes seeing things far beyond where I sat, her raven hair blowing softly about her face.

She said she saw a White Buffalo on a frozen field of snow watching over someone. She couldn't see the face, but he was dark and had big eyes. He was saying something to her, but the air was too cold for the words to reach her. She could see his breath on the air, and it was very faint, as if he was dying.

I told her it must be Calvin Blaine's White Buffalo, but she shook her head, still staring away into some other place and time. "No, this is old. I don't know how far back. He's very sad, but it's not about dying." She drifted away for a while, and when she came back she wanted to gather up our picnic and leave. "I don't like what happened to him," she explained as we picked up our basket and blanket. "He was so young."

"What happened?" I asked, half expecting to hear what 1 had always suspected.

"He was left to freeze to death," she replied. "He had something of great value which was taken from him, and he was left to freeze."

I told her about the old Judge and how frightening Mrs. Leftwich had been.

"She knew about the boy," said Marla. "But she couldn't help him."

I thought about my youthful idea of what kind of treasure had been hidden at the old Leftwich place, and my mind opened up to another possibility, one not as romantic as finding that rare stamp that as a boy I was so sure was hidden there.

Maybe those noises and the spooky feelings I had had as a kid were not imagined after all. I wondered what Calvin would have thought if he had known there was a body down that well he parked beside all those years ago. It might have been what the White Buffalo he thought he'd seen was trying to tell him.

Looking at the map of my old country, I trace a line with

my eye across from Roswell to the Trinity Site, where they exploded the first A-bomb, and back to my hometown. Not much more than a hundred miles or so to either one of them, and it occurred to me that the mystery of the old Leftwich place would go on being puzzling.

Calvin was buried in a plot not far from where we ate lunch, next to his father. Mooch Crane and his wife are across the way, and in between, my old next door neighbors, the Magnesses. Their daughter beat me up a lot when I was smaller, but she turned out to be a friend later on. She thought the treasure was money the judge had left, buried by the crazy old woman who used to come see my grandmother.

Money is too easy to explain. It would not be the sort of secret that would bring out the White Buffalo.

There are no easy ways to find road signs for the Sacred Mountain, so you have to watch for everything. Like having lunch on the grave of a young unknown, lost for years down a well on the Panhandle of Texas.

Sheriff John Lovelace never doubted Calvin had tried to miss something on the road that January night. He knew Calvin drank, and he saw the faint hoof prints in the light dusting of snow on the highway.

He also knew that the person in the well was from another time, and was a stranger to those parts. Whatever happened out on the Leftwich place back then would remain a closed book to anyone but those who had been there.

The track of the Great White Being is difficult to find and hard to follow. You sometimes have to listen to blacksmiths or singers from Argentina to find even a hint of where the Road begins. They show up any and everywhere, but you have to learn to see what you're looking at.

Maria saw the White Buffalo and knew what it was. She knew I was in love with her but didn't find it necessary to say anything about it, and then disappeared not long afterward, back to the pampas of Argentina. I don't think she ever was with Luis or any other man. No one could stand to have their soul looked right through by those dark, sad eyes.

She smiled when I mentioned the UFO crash in Roswell, but she would never go there with me.

She may have been a Buffalo Woman, for all I know.

The Slip Shift

The Last Woody in British Columbia

We got off the train in the middle of nowhere in British Columbia, and there it was, a 1931 Ford station wagon, wood paneling and all. It sat on its own graded dirt road that ran back a mile into the wilderness, where the hunting lodge was located on the banks of the Frasier River. In the distance you could see the snow-covered peak of Mount Robson, the highest point in the Canadian Rockies.

The lodge belonged to a Mr. Fred Armitage. The river and the mountain were God's. The Ford Woody was history and all I could think about while my grandfather and his friend Bill Shirley, his son Billy Bob, and I walked around in the woods that mid-summer of 1954. I hadn't seen the Testarossa Ferrari yet, nor heard anything about the UFO crash in Roswell. I was thirteen and undergoing my own version of a bar mitzvah, old John Wayne-Gary Cooper University version, walking around in the woods with a gun, looking for something to kill.

That, and driving that old Ford up and down the one-mile stretch of rough dirt road that led from the Canadian National Railway line to the lodge. Billy Bob and I took turns running the car back and forth until we probably had put a thousand miles on it.

What I remember is that it wasn't ever run on anything other than that one-mile stretch of road. Mr. Armitage told us he'd bought the car from the Ford dealership in Calgary and put it on a flatcar along with the tractor and blade they used to clear the road to the construction site when they built the lodge.

That always boggled my mind.

A car that had never experienced freedom at all, just leading a drudge's life, slogging back and forth from the railway line to the lodge. It was put up on blocks and covered over during the worst part of winter. A mechanic came at the beginning of the season and serviced the Ford, then came back to put it away for the winter. In that stepping-off-the-front-porch part of my life, that Woody represented all kinds of things to me, and lying by the Frasier River, watching the high white clouds blend in with the snow on the upper reaches of Mount Robson, I dreamed of roaming the country in it. I'd throw a bedroll in the back and set off to see my grandmother's sister in Las Vegas, or go up to New Madrid, where she rode the riverboats with her father. Mark Twain lived in that part of the world when he was alive, and there were people and places there to see and marvel at.

Billy Bob just liked to hear the noise of the engine. He told me it was old and wouldn't make it anywhere. He was more of a pragmatic sort of fellow, and I was having a difficult time maintaining my fantasy about the Woody until he blew the side of the screen porch off with his .35 Remington one evening as we came in from stalking prey in the beautiful wilderness behind the lodge.

My grandfather and Bill praised him for remembering to always point your weapon away from anyone when you were checking it for shells, but that incident put a crack in Billy Bob's psyche, and I guess he decided then and there he'd had it with firearms.

Stephen Sears came along in my life on down the road, a city boy from Chicago who didn't know anything about firearms, who was assigned to my outfit in Viet Nam. He was the first one I'd crossed trails with since Billy Bob in 1954 who could not quite get the hang of unloading a gun. Sears, nicknamed Rodent, was a nice guy, but he never was able to successfully clear his weapon without discharging it. He fired off his .45 into the clearing barrel one afternoon on his way in to battalion headquarters, and the Provo Marshall, who was just on his way out when he heard it, dived into the gutter beneath his jeep.

Gutters in the city of Saigon were usually full of some

dreadful things, and the Colonel was not pleased with the situation. Rodent ended up pulling duty in one of the metal guard towers that surrounded the new MAC-V compound, until Tet came. The city boy from Chicago proved to everyone that he had a difficult time with weapons-clearing procedures, but he won the Silver Star for gallantry when it came time for someone to try to rescue his wounded companions. I heard later that Billy Bob got into the Judge Advocate General's Corps, where he never touched weapons at all, and spent almost all of his time court-marshaling G.I.'s who'd gotten into trouble in Viet Nam.

I never thought at the time of all the enemies we had, but there were plenty, some of them dressed up in friendly suits and spouting friendly things. They weren't in a class with the NVA or VC, but they were dangerous just the same.

Like the CBS camera crew who went against our warnings and got stuck down a narrow side alley near BOQ 3 in Saigon, which ended up getting some pals of mine killed. It didn't occur to me at the time that it was just business. They were setting up their careers on the dead bodies on the TV screen.

Scooping, they called it.

They were still scooping when we moved in to try to get the dead and wounded out of the alley and into the APC, and they went on scooping throughout Tet, nattering and clamoring away, leaning in close to ask some scared kid under fire another stupid question. In my heart of hearts, I committed murder almost daily, but there was always something that kept me from hitting the fire-bar on the .50 caliber machine gun mounted on the truck. I carried a luck piece with me then, given to me by friends at my last party in Fort Dix, New Jersey, before I shipped out. Ernest Hemingway recommended that a young man going away to a war should go equipped with a luck piece that worked. Mine was a champagne cork whipped with stout cord, and it was a dandy. At the time, I attributed everything to it that I now attribute to the Cosmic Boss. Years later I took that luck piece and left it on Ernie's grave up in Ketchum, Idaho, as a way of saying thanks, pal.

It was too hot for ghostly figures of white buffalo, although there were buffalo there, of the water variety, the local tractors to handle the rice paddies. I didn't know Billy Bob was there almost at the same time I was, but I did know I was there, however unreal it seemed, stunned and amazed that I would see the same two Buddhist monks every day on the way to their duties.

They did not seem overly perturbed. Becky, the Captain's driver's friend, thought they were spies and traitors who would use any manner or method to lure the unsuspecting into the same old show. Once they were lulled into carelessness, they would be robbed by the street cowboys and their weapons sold for a healthy profit on the black market.

Life went on day by day, and I saw the same monks walking the same road, and the same war seemed to drone endlessly on, sometimes like a nagging headache that wouldn't go away. Other times it erupted across the landscape like one of the 122 mm. rockets you could see coming from a mile away, which had shrapnel as big as Volkswagens. I talked to my friend Roess about the monks whenever we passed them on the way to get fuel at the downtown motorpool. All he would say was that as long as we were seeing them, nothing bad would happen.

We didn't see them on the 31st of January, 1968, but my mind was elsewhere, and I didn't remember Roess's warning, and he was gone, flown back to The World two weeks before. He was one of the Battalion T.I.s, or traffic investigators, working alone, and had access to a lot of Saigon that most of the other G.I.s didn't have. He'd made friends all over and had a girlfriend he stayed with any time he could in the Cholon district. She was a pretty girl named Lei who worked at the big PX in Cholon. Roess talked about taking her home, but they both knew it was a lie, and that once he'd rotated back, that would be the end of it. She moved on to the next in line, a T.I. from Alfa company.

80

He was at her house the night Tet came, and they didn't find him for a week, shot to ribbons in the alleyway behind her compound. We didn't see Lei again for a long time. When she showed up at our newly reopened club months later, she had a fragile, haunted look that I had begun to see in every face.

Billy Bob had it the night he narrowly averted killing anyone at Fred Armitage's hunting lodge up on the Frasier River back in 1954, and Rodent was wearing it too, the morning he ran back and forth to the wrecked and burning deuce-and-a-half under fire, dragging the wounded and dead out of the alleyway that ran alongside BOQ 3. Lei lowered her eyes whenever any of us tried to talk to her and reluctantly took the money we collected for her, which Tiger said was sent to her little brother, who had gone to live with a cousin in Hue, where she thought he would be safer.

Like the Cholon PX where she had worked, there was nothing much left of Hue that was undamaged. Six thousand United States Marines fought off 20,000 NVA troops in a brutal, bloody campaign that ran on for days, and the beautiful capital city was destroyed. Her brother disappeared along with thousands of other civilians, murdered by the NVA. Our battalion, numbering 1,200 men at full strength, suddenly found itself confronting a division of VC and NVA. For the better part of two days, we weren't sure we were going to see another sunrise.

I know exactly how they felt defending the Alamo.

And I remember distinctly seeing small, brilliant specks of light darting around the heavens above us when the sky wasn't full of magnesium flares or tracer rounds, the tracks of some sort of cosmic sightseers, come to watch the big show on the blue marble called Earth.

I didn't begin to put two and two together for a while longer, and the oddly bent story on the back page of the paper about the incident in the New Mexico desert was still a dim light in the long hallway ahead.

When I stop to think of it, I had seen those same mysterious bright specks out over Mount Robson in British Columbia, lying out in the back of that old Ford Woody along the banks of the Frasier River in 1954. That hadn't been too long after the crash of the UFO near Roswell, so it could be quite possible it was friends of whoever was aboard, out looking to see what had happened to the doomed ship.

There is a simple code in a combat zone, and that is, you never leave your dead or wounded. It might be a common bond we have with someone from across the vast prairies of space. I like the idea that some of their compadres had come looking for them when no one called home.

On the Plain of Reeds

It rolls off your tongue when you say it. The Plain of Reeds. They grow rice there, and it's been one of the places in Southeast Asia where there has always been fighting, because the earth is fertile, and you can grow food. The Chinese and the Plain of Reeds. Tojo and the Plain of Reeds. Renault and the Plain of Reeds.

Winchester Arms and the Plain of Reeds. The Chinese, the Japanese, the French, the Americans, those are only the most recent. You name the scuffle, and it will have always involved the Plain of Reeds.

There was rubber to be had, not too far from the Plain of Reeds, and off the coast in the South China Sea, there's oil. The deadly mix in a faraway, exotic place. Draws big industrialized countries like flies to honey, and then the fun begins.

I've always liked the name because it sounds like the sort of place a UFO would be highly likely to put down. Not crash, like the one outside Roswell. They were probably coming to check out the Trinity A-bomb test site, out on the Jornada del Muerto. Aptly named. Journey of Death. Full of Indians in the old days, and always likely to dish out a sudden thunderstorm with lightning and big wind, like the one that got the Sky Riders. The Plain of Reeds would have been easier to handle for someone unfamiliar with the territory. Only they were road-testing the A-bomb in the Valley of Fire, in the New Mexico desert, getting ready to take the world a little closer to the brink.

Or so they've said. I came across a book once called *The Jesus Factor*, put out by religious fanatics, stating that the bomb didn't actually work when they dropped it on Japan. They came up with an idea that they just fire-bombed the place, then scattered radioactive dust all over the site. That's an intriguing phenomenon, looking right in the running lights of reality, and coming up with a new twist. Revised history making a big-time play. The peaceniks rattling around with their version, and the hawks setting up their own agenda. It was always a lot easier to deal with that sort of thing when there was an actual enemy slinging lead your way, because you had no question about where you stood, and everything was right down to check-your-shorts now.

Not that it was a mistake to have dropped the bombs, because it was another ballgame back in 1945. The world had been at war for years, and we were staring down the barrel of 500,000 more American casualties if we'd had to invade Japan. In that light, the bombs made good sense. Sad, but true. Looking at all the factors, there don't seem to be too many competent players from any government anywhere who would be getting a gold star on their blackboard. The pity of it all is that the ordinary Joe and Susie are always the ones who pick up the tab. Lord Acton was right when he declared that all great men are bad men.

I can't think of anyone from the world of government or high finance that I'd like to go to dinner with, or maybe shoot a game of pool with at an old-fashioned joint like Rusty used to run in Texico, New Mexico. The smoke was so thick you'd have to lean down to table level to see who was there, and the rattle of the dominoes from the back room was almost enough to throw you off your game, but you didn't have to worry about being interrupted for a few hours in the afternoon.

I learned from Pete Rundell about the art of throwing a hook in someone's shot by creating a diversion. Pete's was the glass eye he got courtesy of the Korean War, complete with an American flag. He also had one made up with a naked girl, and another with the logo of his service station. Highly independent sorts seem to take a liking to those wild, out-on-the-fringe places like where I grew up.

No one to mind your business, other than a few nattering

old women who always seemed to know everything, but it was harmless enough. Pete knew Calvin, and they were in Korea about the same time, but Pete got hit and sent home before Calvin saw the White Buffalo. Pete never saw it, and I never heard him mention anything about the Sacred Mountain, except that he'd come to grips with a truth or two while he was in the army, which is probably why he was buried with his naked-girl glass eye, just to shake up the folks who had come by to pay their last respects. The most important one, he'd expounded, was that you leaked if you got shot.

I thought about that once in a while, especially when they'd hang out a line of magnesium flares at two in the morning, and you've have plenty of time to do a little sweating and looking and worst of all, thinking. Odd, what you see by flare-light. Like those faint hoof prints in the light dusting of snow on the Llano Estacado, silvery-black, and moving like a shadow lit from inside itself. Pete ran his service station until he died, shooting snooker most afternoons, always looking for a sucker he could fool with the old roll-the-glass-eye-down-the-table trick. Like old cowboys sitting on the corral watching some young buck get thrown over the top of the barn. They knew how to ride, but they didn't have to prove it anymore.

Sometimes on one of those crystal-clear nights that happen ever so often, you could see all the way to the Plain of Reeds from atop one of the high steel guard towers around the new MAC-V compound. That was where General Westmoreland had his war room and the Big Board. We'd climb a tower where a friend was on duty and smoke and talk while we kept a lookout. You'd see tracer rounds flying from miles away, and then a long time later, like a faint echo, you'd hear the rattle of gunfire. Those nights up in one of the tall armored towers, you were closer to heaven than you'd like, and you could look out over the vast panorama of Saigon, and the river, and on away into the distance toward Laos and Cambodia. We saw a lot of strange things on more than one occasion, but we sat and smoked in silence, with no need to mention something as oddly ordinary as what must have been UFOs down for, as we put it, their nightly fix. Just like watching the tube. Tune in at six o'clock for the war in your living room. This was all before I really learned about Roswell, or the White Buffalo, or the Sacred Road. Sometimes it seems that too much information too soon is as cruel as having it too late. I liked the balance of the Orient, life just passing by, breath by breath, like the river flowing on into the dark sea.

Stories from the Plain of Reeds ran something like that.

Nothing much changed in the scenario, just another batch of actors coming onto the stage. But that name would grab you. That and the Street Without Joy. Who could have thought that up except someone who had been there. The odd thing is that once you've been there, you suddenly are different, even if you didn't know that was the address you were headed for. It is certainly one that you come across on more than one occasion when you finally realize you're on the road to the Sacred Mountain.

Arkin and the El Coyote

We'd go to the El Coyote for Mexican food, then slip on down to the Beverly Cinema to watch Marlon Brando as Rio in "One-Eyed Jacks" every time it played. There's nothing like the big screen, with soda spilled on the floor and cardboard popcorn boxes flying like frantic bats across the theater, to really get you in touch with the true movie experience. It made me remember Tom Mix and Roy Rogers on Saturday afternoon matinees, when twenty-five cents would buy a ticket and another quarter would get you a big orange drink, with popcorn and candy. The Border Theater was the most important building in my small town until the bowling fad hit, and everyone switched their loyalty to Clara's Cafe and went in for bowling shirts with business names on the back, and your own bowling ball.

Drive-in movies were flourishing, too, and what brought it all back in a heady rush was the Beverly Cinema, sitting in the dark cool of the theater, watching Brando looking exactly like Roy Rogers, playing Rio, the dangerous renegade taking a diamond ring off an innocent young girl while he and his partners are robbing the bank. He was such a slick, evil sort of bad guy, with good looks and a load of charm. We've all known someone like Rio. Such a shame that they never did anything worthwhile with their lives.

Brando understood that when he made that film back in the early sixties. Karl Malden and Ben Johnson were brilliant as well, with Katy Jurado, and a Mexican movie star named Pina Pellicer. It was Greek theater at its best, with a man who had been lost and worthless converted and touched by love, who found himself and gave up his old ways and life. And it was tragic, for what starts by the gun ends by it.

What goes around comes around. Whatever you put out, you get back tenfold.

My friend David Arkin knew that movie line by line, and we would have to sit far apart, because I couldn't stand it when he would repeat all the parts himself. He would get completely beside himself with some of the lines that were particularly good. He was a perfect film buff, and loved the movies, and a fine comic and actor, with a gift of handling a pen as well. He had an Emmy for a show called "Storefront Lawyers" back in the early seventies.

I met him at the Old World Restaurant one night, sitting talking to strangers about ashrams in upstate New York. Tender Teddy was telling us about being five years sober and thinking about suicide.

That first night Arkin told me he'd been thinking about killing himself because he couldn't stop drinking. That's a hell of a thing to have to think about, and something I was familiar with. I had thought about sucking on the end of a .45 myself, to quieten the booze and drug demons and the ghosts from Viet Nam, but that had begun to subside by the time we sat in the Old World. I introduced him to my pal Annie, who commented later that all she needed in her life was one more angry young man in a black leather jacket.

They were married three months later, and lasted for eight years. That's when she called to tell me he'd put a hose in his car exhaust and rolled it up in his window. He'd taped it to make sure.

I used to think there were worse things than going on with a life that had lost its meaning. I'm not sure death is such a bad thing. Who can walk in someone else's shoes and know what it's like? Arkin had gone to interview Charles Manson more than once, because he was working on a book about the murder and trial, and thought that was the reason for his sister's cancer and death.

He was a moral man, with a code so strict it killed him, but no one could take away the fact that he knew all the lines out of "One-Eyed Jacks" and could make you laugh with his wry comic's madness.

That's what always strikes me about this business. It's always the small, silly things that get your attention and bring you back to the idea that maybe there's more to it all than a good portfolio and a couple of expensive cars to sit in the garage of the expensive house. Going to El Coyote was one of those things that would loosen Arkin up. Though the food was nothing to speak of, it was close to the Beverly Cinema. Going from El Coyote to see an old film brought the present into stark focus.

Hollywood crucified Brando for that film. No one was ready for anything other than Gary Cooper or John Wayne westerns. I don't know how they overlooked the part Wayne played in "The Searchers," tracking down a white girl captured by Indians to kill her "for her own good." In the end, he is transformed by love. It is a powerful film, and it has a powerful message. That was what was doing Arkin in. He could not stand to see the Beasties winning, or seeming to win.

I wasn't so sure in those years there in L.A. about what it all meant. It was like an advanced course in the absurdity of meaning. If I knew I was going to be sent on a mission behind enemy lines, I would take my training in L.A. Just living there toughens you up for almost anything. You are forever dangled just out of reach of the gold ring. One more round and you'll have it, that's the idea. Death by pin prick. Dripping water slowly on the forehead until you can't take it anymore. Being raised in the wilderness of the Llano Estacado also helped, because there was such a great emptiness there. You learned to fill up your space. Like having your photograph taken next to a house or car or tree. And hats. Everyone wore hats then, to keep from flying off from under your head in the strong prairie winds.

I remember standing in the street with my friend Scott

waiting for a limo from A&M Studios, wondering how I'd gotten there from wherever it was I was before, right in the midst of the Tate-LaBianca murder scare. Nobody had found out about Charlie Manson yet, and it wasn't unusual for a drunken Vietnam vet to be riding shotgun for a rock-'n'-roll star in Hollywood. It made perfect sense. From Barney's Beanery to the Rain Check, everything was in order.

Tim Scott was one of Los Tres Coyotes, who came to the ranch where we'd holed up for Scott to do his album, and it was not unusual to look out over the concrete landscape up to the Santa Monica Mountains or the Hollywood Hills and think of what it all meant. In early 1969 there was enough cosmic upheaval to go around, and when Ned Wynn showed up to meditate outside where Scott was laying down tracks on "Stained Glass Morning," it confirmed that we must at last be on the right track, whatever that was, and wherever it led.

Henry Lewie knew where it led, and that was to a strange piece of "lint" on an otherwise clean track that Eric "Doctor" Hoard had laid down behind Scott's twelve-string. It drove Henry mad for two days, cutting and recutting the same riff that David Anderlee wanted in. It was a layman who finally caught the drift of what was up and suggested that one of the very sensitive mikes might be picking up Ned Wynn chanting outside the building, concentrating on bringing good vibes to the session.

Sure enough, Henry checked, and there was Ned sitting crosslegged just outside where they were recording, thumb and forefingers touching to make the connections, chanting away in a low monotone. Once he was asked to move a little further away from the house, the recording was clean as a pin , and they went on to wrap it.

Maybe the Cosmic Boss works that same way with this session we call life, working around the "lint," slowly cleaning up the track until it's right and tight.

Like paying your dues by eating at El Coyote, even though

you know you're going to get a bad case of heartburn. The Beverly Cinema afterwards is the payoff, when you see Brando looking like Roy, sitting up there on that bank counter eating a banana as pretty as you please. That was a shock. No one had ever thought of doing something like that in a western before. Pistol in one hand, banana in the other, and that slick, charming badness oozing out onto the screen. Arkin and I were coming home late one night from seeing the film there, and he started reminiscing about his life as a boy, playing in the back lots of the big movie studio across Pico Boulevard. I had grown up doing the same thing, only there was no sound lot to explore, and my dreams were a lot further removed than his, but I marveled that night driving back to my joint on Rialto Avenue at how closely we are all related when it comes to the matters of the heart, those most secret of secret dreams.

They are nothing more than faint memories coded into all of us about the Road back, small hints in the dark about what it all means and where we're headed. I never thought much about eating at El Coyote, or how important the Beverly Cinema was, until my friend took his final bow and went to the Green Room.

I saw Jacques Tati there for the first time, astounded how much alike he and my friend Arkin were. David told me he had shown Tati around Hollywood back when and was an avid fan of the French comic genius.

"Ain't it something when the French love Jerry Lewis more than this man?" he asked after seeing "Mr. Hulot's Holiday" one night at the Cinema.

I thought of a scene out of one of Tati's movies, where Hulot was caught upside down in a tree, helpless, watching in quiet horror as his wife came to the window of the house he was trying to sneak into to avoid trouble for being drunk and out late. He was almost safe, but he was betrayed by loose change coming out of his pocket at just the wrong time, clinking loudly enough on the sidewalk below to give him away.

That gave me pause for thought. I wondered how often we're left hanging out there upside down, almost safe, until some small item, a penny or a dime, drops and we're up to it in blazing gunplay again. Maybe that's where the idea of "The Threepenny Opera" came from. It should have been, if it wasn't. I wonder at the zen of El Coyote and the Beverly Cinema and think how odd it is to try to fit that into the scheme of things.

Which you can't without first stumbling across an event that somehow gets your full attention, like the Roswell UFO crash or staring at the tracks of a Great White Buffalo written across the stars. There's a place in all our scripts where those scenes begin.

It's a matter of being ready to show up for the Audition when they make a casting call.

A Taos Artist Story

We were sitting at Cuero's, where they never used to have sour cream, talking about old Taos artists, when I remembered John Young-Hunter. My first wife's father ran a joint in Canyon, Texas called the Panhandle Plains Historical Museum. One of the best things about my first marriage was my wife's father, who knew a lot of interesting people. We had been just kids when we married and didn't know any better, but I got a lot out of the experience, even if her father did say that John Kennedy got just what he deserved that November day in 1963. Most of the time her dad was as enigmatic as a Brahma bull under a salt cedar tree, and no one ever got a real read on him, except that I saw him in action in Taos, New Mexico, talking to the widows of the famous painters that had taken a fancy to that magical part of the country.

There is no other place that has light like it, at least not in the United States. Even a gold rush mentality hasn't completely destroyed it, although at times now it might seem that way. The first time I laid eyes on that country was further back, when I was knee-high, riding in the rear seat of my grandfather's 1951 Chrysler.

We pulled into Taos one late summer day in the middle of a huge Indian pow-wow, and I was gone the minute we got to the motel. My grandfather had to look for me all over town, and my granny was beside herself. He finally found me, dancing on the plaza with one of the groups of dancers who were performing. I had no idea at the time what it all meant, but they were kind and allowed my child innocence and awe to stand in place of head-clutter attic knowledge. I had walked up to the edge of the Road and looked at it even then, and something of that experience must have gone straight into my being. When I went back years later with my then wife and her father, I felt that same sort of awe and wonder. Even being miserably unhappy, I got something valuable from he experience.

John Young-Hunter's widow, a stately woman, showed us the house and grounds and studio, which was a wonderful place. I was no aspiring painter, but I wished I was so I could have a studio like that.

And the light! The light was the color of the country, pale gold and the browns of the pueblo outside town. It changed during the day and made it seem as though you were always walking in a canvas of one of those old masters.

My then wife was not so concerned with the place for what it was and complained about having to ride all the way from Canyon in the back of her father's International Travelall. She was already gearing up for action a year or two later, when she turned me in to my local draft board, run by one Eunice Petersen. Eunice was a spinster and hated kids, and she was in a perfect job in 1965-66, for she was the power-that-was in the case of all young men of draftable age. My friend Karly, who had two stainless-steel knee caps from a bad car crash, got the word, and they hauled him away to do time in Southeast Asia driving trucks. Eunice couldn't wait to tell all us poor bastards who had to come back and re-register who had made it and who hadn't. The look in her eye as she mentioned the names of the dead from Parmer County was like what Dracula must have looked like at the moment he bit into a neck.

That was a long time ago, and the path that led to the Sacred Mountain looked a lot more like the road to Canyon, Texas, long and flat, without the faintest hope of a glimpse of anything any higher than a grain elevator. There were plenty of them. I heard it said once that my Uncle Penrod had enough grain in a single place to feed Sweden for a year.

Eunice and my then wife would come to be close allies, although I didn't know it at the time, walking through John Young-Hunter's studio, looking around for a leftover muse

94

who might still have a little life, if not for painting then surely for the jotting down of some wonderful tidbit that I could use to cash in on the artist's fortune and fame. We spent a lot of what I called "cold time" on that trip, lying in bed barely inches apart, yet further away from each other than if we had been on opposite ends of the earth. That was hard time. It always seemed like gunplay or scuffles on the outside were a lot easier to handle than that particular brand of Chinese water torture.

I had no idea about the Road, or that there might be a map, or that we were all fellow travelers bound for the same destination, whether we were aware of it or not. Anne Arreyo gave me a faintly recognizable clue by drinking everyone in the band under the table one night in a semi-cowboy twist club. Thrown through the plate glass window by a bull rider and coming to in the back of Anne's truck somewhere on the outskirts of Borger, I had glimpses of vast open prairie sky and heard a noise in my head that sounded like one of the old herds of buffalo running, when their numbers were so great that they might fill up the whole horizon as far as the eye could see.

Anne was sitting on the tailgate smoking when I came to. I had a lump on my head, and my entire body ached, but I wasn't cut to ribbons,. She had dragged me out of the worst of the brawl that had erupted between the Nehru-suited mods and a drunk and rowdy bunch of rodeo cowboys who had showed up thinking Ferlin Husky was playing the club.

"Don't get so drunk you can't duck," she said simply. She was a cowgirl from South Dakota and knew those things.

That was cosmic.

But I was doomed to repeat my folly, and forgot her good advice, which was meant for real punches or for worse, death by pinprick. I forgot to duck one night after another wild party at my friend Roy's house, and my free life came to an end when I was bushwhacked by my first wife and dragged out of that renegade artist's world. I was snatched into a volatile mix of sprayed-stiff hairdos and fashion merchandisers bent on going to work for a department store chain in some big city. The flaw in the works was my wife's father, who knew all the famous widows in Taos and put me to work for him that summer. Mrs. Young-Hunter didn't like my then wife, and said so, but truth does not bite very deeply into the thick, self-absorbed skin of a nineteen-year-old. She clucked her tongue and wagged a finger at me after everyone else had left the room, preparing to go to the car.

"You should never allow yourself to be caught up in a snare so easily," she said, watching the retreating figures of my father-in-law and his daughter. "Boone is a wonderful organizer, and I trust him with John's work. There are galleries in New York who want my husband's pictures and are willing to pay nicely, but I would never be able to sleep at night." She pushed open the screen door and swept me out onto the sidewalk with a small, quick motion of her hand. "Don't let your wings be clipped," she clucked, and was gone before I could reply.

My then wife was waiting in the back seat of the Travelall, staring angrily. "That old woman had been drinking," she snapped as I got in. "I don't know what people see in her."

I knew but didn't say, just sat thinking about the startling, clear eyes of the man in the self-portrait that hung above the mantel in the living room, wondering what Mrs. Young Hunter had looked like as a young woman.

My friend in Cuero's was an art dealer and told me of buying that very painting at an auction years later. As we sat pondering why the restaurant didn't serve sour cream, he told me of going back to Taos to visit the Young-Hunter restoration committee, which was responsible for redoing the house and studio where the artist lived. Bob walked up to the mantel where I had admired the self-portrait years before and saw the outline of what had been hanging there. He told them he had the picture and brought it in. It fit exactly, and they bought it on the spot.

Perfect closures.

Like Anne Arreyo, sitting on the tailgate of that pickup on the outskirts of Borger in 1961. She told me one of the facts of life, about not getting too drunk to duck, and also told me about seeing the flying saucers one summer when she was a girl on her family ranch. I remembered staring out over the back fence at my grandfather's, and knew it was the same prairie that ran straight up from where I was to South Dakota. If you had the luck, you might see something like that, but I didn't think about it all that much until later.

Ernest Hemingway was the one who taught me about luck. I followed his prescription for going off to war with a working luck piece given by friends. Mine held up to the test and brought me safely, although not sanely, home from Viet Nam.

Putting buffalo grease on your shield to protect you from White-Eye bullets also works if you believe. He had a hint or two about the Road, only he didn't call it that. You read him, and the way the stories work on you in the end is how Hemingway tugged you toward the Road. I never was sure if he knew where it was he was going himself, but he was blunt and forthright and told you exactly how it was.

Who was there, what the weather was like, and what happened. That always works.

I have learned to not get too drunk to duck, and that there are perfect closures in an imperfect world, if you know where to look and have a little luck.

Pissarro and Pirates

Long trips on motorcycles give you loads of time to think, watching the road roll by. Magic carpets must have done the same for the old seers in the desert. Oceans and deserts overwhelm you with the vastness of their presence and encourage the mind to fill up the space with something, even if it's coming from inside the memory bank. Now, having breakfast in the same restaurant where I watched the storm, I'm thinking of my friend David Arkin, sitting in the Old World in Beverly Hills, talking to a man with a huge head who had been to an ashram in upstate New York. There was talk of the Road to the Sacred Mountain, but it was the odd sort of news you'd pick up in an off-brand service station somewhere in Mississippi, as doubtful as the age of the fuel you'd pumped.

Then we got to the good part, about mothers, who play an important part in the sequence of affairs, since they're part of the travel arrangements. Arkin's mother Eileen was a Capricorn and a wonderful lady. But she was Arkin's Mom. She and her brothers made a dedicated stab at drying out my pal, but even being isolated in the Baja could not deter him from finding the juice. It took Sydney Corbet to come and sit quietly in his living room to convince Arkin that he might be able to make it.

I like the odds of one in ten. That's the going line on an alcoholic or addict being able to quit drinking or drugging. There are no odds like no odds. The sure bet, the money in the bank, the complete measure of an impossible task. Everyone has his time marked, just like the kid in Viet Nam who lay down over the sandbags and whispered his life away. There was no reason it shouldn't have been me who caught the round, but it wasn't.

Here I am, and he isn't. Not on this plane, anyway. We go

on, but there's a lot of playing fields in this neck of the cosmos. My friend Bruce Cobb was a fighter ace in World War II and a skillful sailor and played first clarinet for Benny Goodman, but that didn't keep the VW bug from rolling off its jack and crushing him without fanfare in his garage one Sunday morning in Charlotte Amalie.

A ticket out.

He showed me the sea road to the Sacred Mountain. I grew up on the high plains, and although it had all been covered by an ocean at one time, there was nothing more than the tailwater of irrigation wells by the time I arrived on the scene. Candide Church bought an Alan Gurney-designed ocean racer for the SORC and had it built in Poole, England. *I'll Do* was a great pumpkin seed, forty feet long with a seven-foot draft. She carried 1,200 square feet of spinnaker, which was the first sail I had to learn to handle on my apprenticeship aboard. It was as awesome to watch that chute pop and fill as it was to hear a Cobra start a pass on an enemy position. Bruce was a good teacher and always kept calm, telling you what you did wrong and what to do to correct it, even though he might be walking on the outside of the lifelines after taking a knockdown. "Look to it, lads! Cut that sheet, quickly!"

This while the big spinnaker was slowly filling with water, threatening to drag the boat turtle. Which means stick down. Mast straight down. Situation desperate. His starched white sailing shorts and shirt were creased, his silvery pilot's sunglasses reflecting our terrified faces, as he quietly got us to get ourselves out of the jam. On the way back to port, he gave us the rundown of all our mistakes, promising to take us out the next day to practice flying and taking down the big, very intimidating sail, which could take the boat up to twelve knots in the right conditions, which felt like a barely controlled speed-wobble on a fast motorcycle.

It got your attention.

Like the Pissarro Building on Main Street, where Messrs.

Isadore and Ralph Paiwonsky grew up. It had been home to the artist who had started the Impressionist movement in France, and I could feel his ghost every time I was in the building. Looking out at the harbor from the front porch where he painted as a young man, I could see his paintings through his eyes. It was like being transported, just as sailing on *I'll Do* showed me a face of the sea l could never have experienced in any other way. Shoulder down, she raced through the Atlantic and Caribbean in all sorts of weather short of a full hurricane. Thoughts of Ishmael in a cramped whaling boat in the Southern Oceans not only came to mind but were felt in every straining nerve in my body, watching as we tacked back and forth up the Narrows or roared out downwind, rolling on toward Red Hook or Charlotte Amalie.

Mr. Isadore told me of the pirate ship *La Trumpuse*, along with many other yarns of the islands that he had kept safe from being forgotten. Jim Knud-Hansen had pictures on the walls of his father's house of scenes from the early days in St. Thomas before they were all stolen and sold by people who crashed there during the years it was known as Hippie Haven. That was where Karen Snyder lived for a time when she first came to the islands, and where she was living when I developed one of those unexplainable crushes on her. She was playing and singing where my friend One-Eye Bobby was tending bar. I latched onto being in love with her like I'd latched onto the girl Nicole in Sydney the year before, when I'd gone there on an R&R from Viet Nam.

There wasn't much left in my world in May of 1968, and I was bordering on the last jump off the Big Circus Wagon before I met the girl in a hotel bar in the Kings Cross district. Friends were dead, I was alive, the war was going on still, and I wasn't due to rotate back to The World for another three months. Stepping off that plane in Australia was one of those things in life that deliver you from yourself, just like crossing trails with Karen Snyder in Charlotte Amalie a year later. There was no

100

music or magic just the simple, kind touch of another human being that did it. I wasn't even aware of what had happened until I left to fly back to Viet Nam on that last day of the R&R. I can still recall getting into the cab at Nicole's front doorstep, looking out over Sydney Harbor, and the emptiness that began to come back as I rode away. I had not even realized that it was gone, that she had filled up that place that was filled with darkness and death. No one had told me then that there would be moments on the Road like that, when it felt like death itself, only worse, for it was there, and it wasn't ended. There was no relief from the pain, and no one had explained to me back then that pain was the messenger, not the message.

I can't recall when I got that, but it was not in Sydney, nor that first time in Charlotte Amalie. The explanation was Nicole, then Karen Snyder. And she died before not much more time had passed, from an overdose of uncut heroin. All her youth and beauty had not spared her from that. When I went to her funeral that summer, she was simply one more death added to the growing number of faces of those who were not around anymore.

One-Eye Bobby told me about it at our "breakfast club," where the bar-keeps gathered at the Gate or the Captain's Table. He'd been a horse user before, when he'd lost his eye. He chipped now and then, but had been straight for a while, since the rumor had gone around of some dangerous supplies of the drug being funneled through the islands. I took the news hard. It jolted me to think as I sat there over my Bloody Mary that the beautiful young singer had had troubles enough to look for solace in heroin. He told me she had needle marks in both her arms, behind her knees, and on the tops of her feet, sign of an addict who's been shooting up so much they can't find a good vein to fix.

Karen had been one of those who crashed at Jim's Hippie Haven and stole antiques from his historic house to buy the very thing that had caused her death at the tender age of twenty-three. Bruce Cobb helped at the time by taking me out on *I'll Do* and telling me stories of flying off the deserts of North Africa to escort the bombers over Italy, and of traveling with Benny Goodman's band before he went into the service. Just like Top, talking about fishing in Georgia to take your mind off a slug floating around with your name on it.

I didn't know what was going on, but I sensed it was something big, and it helped the open wounds to mend enough that I didn't die from them. There was a part of me that understood something about the nature of the Road, like looking at a reflection of an object in a glass. It was like the real thing, but it was not real.

Those fragile illusions, like the image of life, a faint white cloud floating against the blue sky, nothing but a whisper from eternity, and here for such a short time.

Mr. Isadore filled me with yarns of the pirates who used to call St. Thomas home, liking the natural harbor, and the greedy governors who sat in charge of them, always willing to look the other way if a person was able to pay enough. *La Trumpuse* was captained by one such man, who had used the island as a home port until the then governor decided he would take the vessel and all the loot instead of merely a cut. The captain heard of the double-cross, and rather than surrender his ship, he scuttled her and escaped. Twenty years later, a volcano erupted close by, and *La Trumpuse* lay revealed on the glistening mud of the harbor floor, for with the violent upheaval the sea had receded, making those ashore mad with desire for the treasures they had heard she had been carrying. More than a hundred townsmen hurried out onto those tempting mud flats, on fire to get their share of the ill-gotten booty, when the sea returned to claim its own.

A few days afterwards, a big wind spawned in the Caribbean blew in, completing the almost total destruction of the favorite harbor of the buccaneers. Jim Knud-Hansen had had a photo on his wall of a steam packet from Savannah, Georgia, deposited halfway up the highest point of St. Thomas, placed there by the tidal wave from the volcano.

When the terrible storm was finally over, *La Trumpuse* had disappeared from both the sea and the land. Mr. Isadore said his own father described the noise of the ocean and wind as that of a hundred thousand doomed souls wailing, and that he had been washed up from the sidewalk in front of the Pissarro House all the way to the top of the roof of Dr. Knud-Hansen's home, almost a quarter-mile up from the harbor.

I imagined what thoughts ran through the mind of Mr. Paiwonsky Senior, facing a wall of water that loomed up higher than the West Indian Docks. It must have felt pretty much the same as sitting in a jeep that had been shot out from under you, looking down the blackness in an alley lit with the silvery magnesium flare above and seeing the squad of enemy soldiers coming along with their weapons at the ready. The hundred thousand doomed souls wailing could easily have been the spooky gunships working out toward the edge of Tan Son Nhut, or the Phantoms making their runs out toward Cu Chi. It left the same metallic taste in the mouth and made you work hard at being able to spit. Top Shunk had the cure, which was a good ass-chewing about your flak vest being undone, or that you needed to keep a better lookout. What it did was give you something to do besides be afraid.

Left cooking too long, that would take the legs out from under you, and made it dangerous for everyone. Top's recipe was to keep you busy with nickel-and-dime stuff so that you didn't do too much pondering about what it all meant.

Arkin kept slipping off into that, and other than the El Coyote and the Beverly Cinema, there wasn't enough distraction to keep him from thinking about all those things that usually come in the middle of the night, when you're tired and your guard's down. When Syd Corbet died, Arkin was cut adrift, and there wasn't much anyone could do. I wasn't living in L.A. anymore, and Kid Chocolate was overmatched. I was

Kid Bunny, and he was Kid Chocolate. We'd go downtown to the gym to watch the fighters work out, then to the Pantry for a meal that would stay with you for a week. It was a holdover from the Depression, when you might not get to eat for two or three days. We'd come back to Glendon Avenue and lament that there were no more fighters, not in the old definition. No matches going the full fifteen, with the ring slippery from blood. It was hard to figure that into the Road, but it was there, just as surely as the huge bull moose I saw in the late summer one year, standing up to his knees in a pond beside the highway up from Banff to Jasper. It was very early morning, and the pond was covered with a wreath of white vapor. The big bull slowly lifted his head when he heard the motorcycle stop, but I just sat there, hardly daring to breathe, and he finally went back to the business of gathering his breakfast.

It's funny how circles start, then get bigger, and lead away into a distance so far you'd swear it was never coming back, but they always do. I was reading a small book of Hemingway's not long ago, a book I had never heard of before. It was about marlin fishing off Cuba, and I marveled at the details he gave, exactly the weight line to use and the brand name of the rods and reels. He talked of the bait that was the best for each fish, and what to use for the really big fish. I slowly perused the book, noticing the passion he felt, and how he truly did follow his own formula of always writing around a subject. He believed that if you talked about something directly, it would kill it.

A thought that might bear more study, it turns out. The world has gotten into a condition not unlike those unfortunate citizens who lost their lives by being out on the shining mud flats in search of the big easy from *La Trumpuse*. Mr. Isadore Paiwonsky fought progress on the island of St. Thomas from the time he was able to thwart the designs of his brother Ralph, not because he didn't want an improvement in the human condition of the people living there, but because what was being peddled as progress was nothing more than a thin excuse to put in another golf course or fancy hotel and casino.

I liked Mr. Isadore because of his eccentricity, and because he always had an A.H. Riise shopping bag full of his money.

"I'd rather throw it all over the cliff on Tortola than let a bunch of legal leeches start fighting over how it's going to be split up." I never knew how much be carried in the bag, but it was a sum. I found out later he had hired Johnny the Tenor to ensure that nothing happened to him. It was an inspiration, and one that was plainly working.

Pirates had a code and would draw the line if pushed, like the master of *La Trumpuse*. For all the years I knew Mr. Isadore to carry around huge chunks of the Paiwonsky family fortune, there was never a single incident of anyone ever attempting to steal from him. They stole Jim Knud-Hansen's house practically out from under him, but it never occurred to him to hire Johnny the Tenor to keep an eye on Hippie Haven. Jim was a drunk and knew the kids were slowly picking the carcass of the historic old house clean, but it wasn't in his nature to be anything less than courteous, even if it was his home that was being plundered.

I know that what goes around comes around, and that whatever you're putting out, you'll get back ten-fold. Karen Snyder lived at Hippie Haven, and I know she stole some of the antiques from the house and sold them to buy drugs. Another long-term resident thief was a kid who tended bar for a while at the Sand Box. He had been working the night Janis Joplin and Scott and the picker from John Lee Hooker's band, along with the Beach Boys' drummer, played the bar, when the music was so secret and big that it could not have been recorded, even if there had been equipment there on the spot. The kid drowned a few weeks later, and they said it was heart failure due to heroin use. Jim kept opening his door to anyone who asked until the local police chief closed him down.

In the end, there were five people who died from drug abuse, and every one of them had stolen from the gentle drunk Jim. I used to wander by his house long after Karen had died, hoping to maybe hear the notes from her guitar, like in the old days, but the place was dark and bare, full of other older ghosts as well, from when the volcano and big winds had covered Charlotte Amalie with black ash and a wall of water so high it reached halfway up Signal Hill.

Johnny the Tenor couldn't have protected anybody against that natural disaster, but Mr. Isadore and his bag of money were safe on the street. Arkin was gone in a Honda sedan, a small car for a large man, and the El Coyote is the worse for his passing.

You pay to play.

Those kinds of things are easily understood.

Pissarro sat on the verandah of his family home, painting the harbor and the hill behind the West Indian Docks in a way that changed the way the world looked at form and color. A little while later Mr. Isadore walked that same porch with his bag full of money, telling me about the skipper of *La Trumpuse*, refusing to let a thief steal from a pirate.

That alien ship went down outside Roswell. They had probably come to take a peek at what had been going on out in that vast, secret desert. The odds of them crashing after coming all that way were slim to none, but it happened all the same. Great minds are still capable of small mistakes that can sink the boat.

Would the cause have been on their light recorder black box? Did our government learn when they investigated that the pilot had had to take a leak just when the storm hit?

Were their last words, "Oh shit!"

Each small piece of the puzzle must be studied to get the full effect. One day it will all fall into place, and it will be so easy, it'll be hard to believe that it was ever a mystery at all.

Sometimes the Road seems to go nowhere, and it passes through darkened woods, where you aren't sure it will ever come out again.

But it does.

Lightning Strikes

"Lightning struck the Valentines as they stood on an overlook near the entrance to Palo Duro State Park. Jack Valentine's tennis shoes were blown off, and a crater was left where he was standing." (from the *Amarillo Daily News*)

Palo Duro Canyon was always home to strange events, from the dinosaurs to the time when Lionel Ledbetter believed there might be an entrance there into a gigantic underground river that ran beneath the rolling plains. Lionel spent his weekends exploring, hiking up and down miles of washes and gullies, probing and poking into rattlesnake and tarantula holes, frightening necking couples from the local college who had gone to the park to try to find some privacy.

He never found the fabled opening to that vast unseen sea. He graduated and moved away to Kansas, where he taught geology and lamented his failure. Until Jack Valentine came along, no one suspected how close to the truth Lionel had been, only he had not had the last and most sacred key to the mystery, the bolt from the blue, to help him enter that strange kingdom that lay at imagination's end.

Lionel was roaming around the West Texas State campus when I arrived there in 1961, in shock that I wasn't going to a school on the East Coast, dreading the fact that I was having to go to school at all. I had finished a semester or two at another university, then flunked so many courses that I was suspended, which turned out to be a blessing, for my grandfather decided to send me away to look at the world, to finally decide what I was going to do with my life.

That was a confusing question, because there were no real answers to any question being asked. I was in the middle of the country where Calvin Blaine saw the White Buffalo, but the closest thing I got from the university was that their football team was called the West Texas State Buffaloes.

They meant well, and they did their best, but the truth always came from unlikely sources, like Lionel Ledbetter, or a few instructors who had ended up in exile at the tiny campus stranded far out in the middle of the Llano Estacada. When I read the Russians, I felt more closely akin to them than the people in my own surroundings. Gorky's *Lower Depths* was a favorite of mine in those days, and I was perfectly at home in the Zen Bar in Amarillo, which I thought of as some strange way station in Siberia,

Which, oddly enough, was near the truth. I remember staring out across a slate-gray prairie beneath a cold slate-gray sky, standing in my friend Don Callerman's "studio," a converted chicken coop he had sealed by tar-papering the windows and running a long extension cord from a neighbor's house so he could have a small electric space heater to warm himself. He was into very large, wall-sized canvases, with lots of hand-smeared oil effects, and was one of the first I'd seen to strip naked and roll around on his work.

I was rooming at the time with my friend Barry, who had come home from his stint in the army to finish college, and Don managed to come by every afternoon to talk shop and drink all the beer in our refrigerator. He was very good at it, and we let him go on with the hoax, because we liked to watch him work.

"How's it hanging?" he'd ask when he came in, walking toward the kitchen.

"Have a beer, Don," we'd say, knowing that's where he was going anyway.

"Thanks, I might like one at that." Then he'd make small conversation at the refrigerator door, while chugging one beer after another. He never missed a beat in the conversation. Then he would stroll leisurely out with the "one" beer, and sip it while we talked about classes we were taking, or the whereabouts of the parties that would be happening on the weekend. Those parties were our lifeblood, all that made the bleak weekdays bearable. They were looked forward to the way a prisoner looks forward to his release day, spoken of and planned carefully, handed about by word of mouth as one might handle precious jewels.

Don belonged to a group that lived off campus, mostly in Amarillo, seventeen miles away. He had a creaky old Plymouth four-door that was painted in the likeness of a rhino, and he'd motor back and forth looking like Bogart on his boat in "The African Queen." I was always amazed watching him sail down the four-lane, wallowing and yawing like a Chinese junk in a gale.

There was a beauty to it, though, and I can't think of any of the newer cars that would match a soul-longing as well as that Plymouth fit Don. He was painting at a time when Albert Camus had become quite fashionable as an Existentialist, and that proved to be one of the things that saw me through the roughest part of the whole enchilada. Bertie Camus, speaking of the absurdity of it all, took the fangs out of a world that could bite, and bite hard, and was learning to rip the throat out of anyone who limped.

I was limping then, moon-struck and hopelessly in romance with a sorority sister named Jackie, who was going with the president of a fraternity that threw a ball every year. Everyone went as a Southern officer or a belle of the South. I watched Jackie come and go, writing her poems that would make me wince if I had to read them today, pining away next door with my great and wonderful companion cat, a Siamese named Ernie who was the embodiment of Ernest Hemingway, right down to the drinking of cheap Italian wine, and shooting up the commode with my .45 caliber automatic. I don't know what it was that finally made her notice me, but it happened, and I actually got a date with her, not long after the Old South

Ball. We were to go to dinner at one of the nicer places in Amarillo, and I had my ulterior plans of bringing her back to the apartment for a few drinks. Barry was to be away for the night, and it was a weekend, so she didn't have to be back in the women's dorm until one o'clock.

That sounds strange now, having a curfew, but it was rigidly enforced, and they would boot you out of the university if you broke the rules enough times.

I had accounted for everything except how my Siamese cat would react, and there was no explaining to him what to do. My life at that point was not very focused, and any talk of the Road to the Sacred Mountain would likely be of ways to get laid. That much was obvious, when you're young and full of sap.

Heaven in the backseat of a 1951 Ford.

Ernie the Siamese was true to form, waiting patiently until I got Jackie back to the apartment to make his move. I knew when we hit the door that there was going to be trouble, for the cat's ears were down in his water buffalo position.

"Oh, he's cute! What's his name?" She moved toward him as she spoke, and I didn't have the chance to warn her.

Before I could speak, he had grabbed her arm with his forepaws and kicked quickly with his rear, opening up a nasty wound that spurted like a West Texas gusher.

Jack Valentine had probably felt the same at the moment the big volts hit him. Blown right out of his sneakers, just like me, watching Jackie bleed like a stuck pig all over the cheap rug, her eyes rolled back, and that funny little way she had of breathing real jerky just before she screamed.

I had to fill out a lot of paperwork at the emergency room. They thought at first I must have stabbed her, she was bleeding so much, so they called the sheriff's department, and a deputy came by to question me. Jackie was recovered enough by then to tell everyone that I had a vicious, dangerous animal in my apartment that had attacked her without provocation and should be put to sleep.

Mad as I was at Ernie, I didn't want him to be executed over a chick like Jackie. I promised myself to try to get him off the hook so I could make his life miserable for the rest of his days.

Of course he knew when to take a hike, and he disappeared for a while, holed up with one or another of the people who took care of him when he wasn't hoodwinking me. By that time, I had gotten the word that another friend of mine had gone out with Jackie shortly after the cat attack and developed a case of the clap for his trouble.

The girl I had become so enamored with, and written a dozen poems to, had given him VD.

I was so grateful and relieved that I rushed out to find Ernie to thank him. He had kippers for dinner for the rest of the time he spent with me, which was up through my marriage to my first wife. He was smarter than I was there, too, but I didn't listen to him about her, and I lost him.

He went out one night for cigarettes and never came back.

Not that I could blame him, but I envied his approach to getting untangled from a situation that was so bad it was no one's fault we both didn't die from it.

It was one of the many of my first Road signs.

When I look back, it was like traveling a hundred miles an hour through a construction zone on an interstate.

Lionel Ledbetter was looking for that lost entrance to the underground sea, and I was off on my own quest, and just like old Jack Valentine out at the entrance to the Palo Duro, I'd been quietly blown out of my sneakers over and over again without getting the point.

Even on the trip back from Wyoming with Delvin in his body cast, I had been getting messages that were as plain as the big-sky mornings through the pickup window as we sped back down that long road to the Panhandle.

There is more to this than meets the eye, and gargling Jack Daniels at roadside rest stops didn't clear my vision.

At least, not then.

Running Up the Flag

My old friend David "Dago Red" Piccandra told me the story of running up a Texas flag that had flown over the state capital, and the grief it had caused, seeing as how it was Viet Nam. For some reason the enemy gunners took great offense at seeing the Lone Star banner flying so brightly over a hooch in the middle of a base camp.

It drew a lot of fire, and pissed off all his pals, because nobody likes to be the magnet that draws incoming. That's a thing that's true in a combat zone, as well as everywhere else. Sometimes incoming isn't readily identifiable, but is dangerous, whether you recognize it or not. Maybe Italian blood, maybe not, but it had a familiar ring to my first wife's being able to handle a cut-glass ashtray like a Frisbee and taking me off the couch one night during an argument, after a "flag had been up" about how I wasn't coming straight home after class at the university.

That was a sorely fought battle, as hot and heavy as any lead-slinging in 'Nam, only with a different kind of wound and body count. The real firefight was a lot more honest, and you always knew where you stood. Bloodletting in close in-fighting with a significant other is often more brutal and cruel and leaves scars that last at least as long. I admit I didn't know anything then about how to do anything other than copy my John Wayne-Gary Cooper University role models, and no one else did either. It took a long time to figure out that every time you sat at table saying "I don't know" as an explanation, you got a barbed-wire enema. If you wanted something different to happen, you had to behave in a different way.

Like Delbert, pissing on the electrified fence, it only took a few jolts to find out there were a lot of other fun things to do in the world besides finding new and more intense pains to experience.

No Road signs showing up there in those times, though, or there probably were, but I was still too blind to see them. It was cruel to have to know something for a long time before you could do anything about it. Like sitting Stateside, thinking about something that happened a long time before in Viet Nam.

There didn't seem any rhyme or reason to it then, but now I can see the dance, like a great wave at sea, moving in a very predictable way, moving with silent purpose, always toward the shore. I was always looking for the pieces to the puzzle, but the puzzle was that every single piece was a part of the whole, and it could not be experienced in any way other than full bore.

It was.

It became.

It passed, and is passing.

Running up the flag.

It always draws fire, and it always gets the blood stirred up. Listening to a lone piper at Dryberg Abbey in the County of the Borders in Scotland, I sat straight up in my bed, my heart pounding and my emotions completely scrambled. I wanted to sob, or fix bayonets and go over the parapet, following the young subaltern through the wire toward the machine guns, who was talking low to the lads and kicking a soccer ball in front of him as lightly as you please. I actually met him, but not in Flanders. It was Viet Nam in 1968, and he earned the nickname "Bullet." He was a good officer and didn't need his insignia pinned to his collar to make you respect him. He was running up the flag in his own way.

Gerald Waltman.

I don't think he'd mind my calling him by name. He had a twin brother, and they were both in the army. The last time I saw Lt. Waltman was during Tet of '68, when he and a kid named Jefferson were wounded in some fierce fighting around a place we called BOQ 3.

Bachelor Officers' Quarters in plain lingo. It was a place none of us would forget. There are thirteen names of my friends on the Vietnam Memorial from that day and others, back in the time warp when that all happened. Running up the flag is like losing your Slip Shift, or as Kurt Vonnegut puts it, "coming unstuck in time."

It's like a single breath ago now. I can see their young faces and hear their laughter at the Rialto Tea House, or sitting in the hooch, reading letters from home, or showing someone the picture of a car they planned to get once they got back to The World. They're locked into a muscle car year now, and it's strange, but those cars still look as good now as they did in those ads back then. Showing up in a GTO or a Ford Shelby was "running up the flag" big-time. The noise those engines made sent shudders up and down your spine whether you were in the car or not.

I wondered what kind of car Lt. Waltman would have gotten, and what ever happened to him. I wondered what happened to all of us until a footnote from the Cosmos fell on my head and I saw the pitch to it. Those lost wanderers from wherever they were from came crashing out of a storm near Roswell for bigger reasons than anyone could have imagined, and when I finally got it, I could see it all a little more plainly.

They came for a look because they wanted to know who was there and what the weather was like.

They were running their flag up, in their own Sky Rider way.

You have to get back a long way away from the canvas to see what the painting is.

Or as Mooch Crane would have put it, tilting his chair back in Rusty's Pool Hall, "Standing too close to the stove will catch your clothes on fire, and you forget about being hungry."

The Talking Typewriter

Tales of the Talking Typewriter

It started out as a joke, but somewhere along the line, it took on a life of its own. Blame it on the Talking Typewriters (heavy, cumbersome mechanical things that were used in the dark ages before the advent of computers), long imprisonment, or the shadows and darkness from the unbroken prairie light that slowly erodes all reason. It (the Talking Typewriter) had been languishing in the attic of Marcus Barnes's house on Main Street for too long, and when it sensed freedom, it ran amok.

In those confusing days, it was too early to see much of any direction, and it took something of great import to catch one's attention. The UFO crash in New Mexico was in the not-too-distant past, but it no longer had the same kind of impact as the assassination of the Prince of Camelot in 1963, or the building social unrest in the United States. And then there was this small thorn that kept cutting deeper and deeper into America's consciousness. It had its own sound.

Viet Nam.

Its name cut like a razor through the newspaper stories and crept across the screens of the newly popular and ever-present TV like a wildfire out of control. It would spread unabated for more than twelve years longer. It's spreading still.

My friend Carter had dug out the typewriter to do a paper for one of his classes at the university, but soon found the beast to be totally unsalvageable as an instrument for assigned schoolwork. All it would do was long, rambling correspondence from dozens of imaginary people, from colonels in the British Army to Reginald, the original all-time worthless bounder, to whores who worked the lower streets below Waterloo Station. Over the years, the Talking Typewriter nattered away. We little realized that he was somehow connected to an omnipresent channel of information, much as automatic writers are tuned in to some cosmic network. There is not much selection, but it is a conduit into some other range of the mind, lost out in the wilderness. Much like what the Sky Riders would have marveled at, looking at the Rockies on some sunrise morning in winter.

But in the time period we're talking about now, there was plenty to occupy the pilgrim, and many diversions running on the same billboard at once. Mooch Crane used to laugh at the new farm machinery that was coming out at the time. He would go down to the Minneapolis-Moline implement dealer once or twice a week to look at the four-row planters or ten-row harrows.

"It'll get to the point all a feller has to do is just hitch up one of these contraptions to the back of that high-dollar tractor, and before he knows it, he'll be planted and harvested all at the same time." He'd chuckle that odd gasp of a laugh to himself, then squint out over the unrelenting grip of the prairie. "If it don't hail."

That was always a great hit with the crowd of men in work clothes gathered at the dealership, men who had lived through the Great Depression and had skin the color of sunburnt earth from long hours of toil at their chosen task of nurturing growing things out of a sometimes less than hospitable environment.

Sometimes the Talking Typewriter would talk of them as well.

The house where Marcus lived had a small apartment behind, and our friend Terry Finley took it during the last days before the ax fell. Critical mass was fast approaching in 1965, and the "times they were a-changin'," as Robert Zimmerman, a.k.a. Bob Dylan, was so aptly putting it. I had been to a party in Greenwich Village and heard this scraggly kid semi-screeching a song at a piano and could only think of throttling him so I could talk to the raven-haired beauty standing next to him, but nothing happened, except that I had a few more drinks and quietly wandered around heartbroken in the Village.

I was in the Village again a year later, a soldier in training at Fort Dix, New Jersey, visiting my pal Al Slagle on West Eleventh, and stumbled into a club that was trendy, and lo and behold, there was the scraggly kid, only he was going by the name of Dylan. Joan Baez, the raven-haired beauty I had seen, was playing there with him, and I wandered around a late-night city again, heartbroken and doomed, for I already was stuck in the "enemy camp" by the very fact that I had been drafted when my then wife turned me in to the local draft board in Parmer County.

Eunice Petersen, the Selective Service secretary there, was delighted.

And so was my ex, who wrote me a note informing me that she hoped I'd lose my legs when she found out I was going to Viet Nam.

Road signs are sometimes difficult to read, when the blood pressure is up. Intense emotional signals tend to cloud the issues, and often a perfectly clear piece of the puzzle will look like no more than one of those cloudless skies at sea, all blue, without a hint as to which direction to go.

I have learned to thank my teachers, and I have had to fall down and kiss my ex's feet for what she did for me back then. At the time, it made a great sympathy-getting story, but as I began to look at the traces of the Trail, I saw it clearly marked right through that part of the geography where we had been traveling together.

Lionel Ledbetter was looking for the hidden entrance to the great Middle Earth, and old Jack Valentine had been bound for glory out on the Palo Duro, while I was doing hard time in a terrible hoax, drifting away into the wake of my ex's life. John Glenn was orbiting the earth while I fought my way up the beach of business ed classes, looking at a future that was as bleak as a photo of the Great Plains in the mid-1930s. My ex was driven, and dragged me along with her, which was lucky, and then when it appeared that I was dead weight, she cut me loose like the albatross I was.

Dragged behind the pickup of the Big Guy again, like an unruly pony tied on behind Charlie Norton's Chevy.

It took a while to know that I could ride in the cab and enjoy the view. It was something the Talking Typewriter said much later, after the emotional gunplay of the divorce had settled down and I was camping in Carter's house on Twenty-First Street. I woke up one morning with a letter from my Selective Service board on my chest informing me I was to report for a physical. With it was a sheet of crisp new typing paper covered with the wisdom of that ancient Remington Rand.

"Greetings!" said the Selective Service letter.

"Hello," said the Talking Typewriter.

"This is your old friend Sparky. You are going to be taken away soon, and I wanted to tell you this, just so you'd know.

"If you don't get this message tonight, you'll be gone soon, and I can't help, except to remind you to think of the moonlight beach, and old Blind Pew coming along behind, counting out the steps to guide you to where the treasure's buried. If they know you're a believer in *Treasure Island* or *The Wind in the Willows*, they'll make sure you are never free again.

The house on Twenty-First Street was my only refuge at that time, and it was rapidly crumbling into the same sort of disarray as watching survivors pour out of a bombed and burning city.

We were all scattered about on a wild prairie wind, blown to the four corners of a darkening world being torn apart at its seams.

Yet the Talking Typewriter kept on talking.

Carter finally told me years later in the islands that he hadn't been the Talking Typewriter. The Remington Rand had done it all.

I had a .45 caliber sidearm in Viet Nam that was made by that company, and it was named Chug. It must have come from the same mold somewhere, for it had become more than a pistol and was largely responsible for my belief in luck pieces in the war.

Those letters from the Talking Typewriter followed me from the high plains to Indo-China and back, to the Islands, Florida, Maine, Virginia, California, the Islands again, and back to the Chihuahuan desert. They stopped when the old Remington rusted up from the high humidity in the Caribbean, and like an old pirate who was laid to rest amid his booty, it was tossed overboard one night in Charlotte Amalie harbor, where the bones of *La Trumpuse* had once rested.

Carter said they had a wake and doused the old boy with libations of Mount Gay rum, and a bugler from the local Coast Guard cutter blew taps for him.

He'd seen the coming and going of standard typewriters that could be used to anchor ships, and the rise and fall of disco. He knew a good thing when he saw it, and knew his days were numbered when it was no longer possible to buy a ribbon for him from an office supply joint. I think he liked the idea that he was buried where the old pirate ship had been scuttled and would be able to sit with the sharks and ramble on about Tennessee Williams and other items of interest, as befits a Talking Typewriter.

They don't make typewriters or newspapermen the way they used to, and I'm not sure that's such a good thing. Progress means you're going somewhere fast, but you're not sure whether it's the right direction or not.

There's still something to be said for strong fingers that can work a standard typewriter, or a hand that can use a pen that's filled from a bottle of ink. In the rush forward, some of the glue that holds it all together has been forgotten, and we can only wonder at what has happened.

It's easy to see how something so clear-cut and simple as the Road is overlooked in the dust. It was that way in my case. I wasn't paying enough attention to Lionel out there searching for Middle Earth, or hearing the call of the New Mexican desert, its rich voice full of yarns that might pull me back from the false trails I'd been following.

Sooner or later, if you're still not listening, you get a tap from the Cosmic Two-by-Four.

Or a disturbing batch of madcap letters from a Talking Typewriter that will track you down no matter where or how far you go.

They always ask you the same thing.

Do you remember who you are?

Where are you, and where are you going?

Have you taken a long look out the front window and wondered what the boys in the UFO were looking for out on the New Mexico desert?

Did they find it?

Have you checked your mailbox today?

Rodeo Philosophy
on an Italian Beachhead

When I wasn't running away from home as a very young pup, I was busy in my grandparents' house, going through my grandfather's drawer where he kept the war trophies that my Uncle Penny had sent him. It was a fascinating place, my grandfather's room, full of forbidden things that no one was to touch. Every time I was caught, I was whipped and admonished never to go near the gun collection, but it was too big a pull, and I couldn't keep myself from going back. There is a dark aura around objects of destruction, and it's impossible to resist. The power of having something in your hand that can kill is seductive, and the feeling it gives that one is now truly strong. My grandfather was a wise man, so after he saw a spanking wouldn't keep me away, he sat me down at the dining room table and I heard the truth. Anything as dangerous as a gun needs to be studied and learned, and he proceeded to start me out on an education in firearms and what responsibilities a man has concerning them. What I heard was straight out of the guide to balanced living. You never point a weapon at anything or anyone you don't intend to use it on. And you don't shoot something you don't use. We would go out with our guns when I was old enough to walk along beside him and carry a rifle or shotgun, but we didn't shoot anything unless we had a need. Sometimes we'd walk for miles out in the sand hills behind our small town, and my grandfather would tell me the lore of the animals we would see, or where they had been. That great inland coastline was a ridge of sand that ran all the way from Muleshoe almost to Portales. The Clovis people had roamed around there back in

123

the twilight of time, and there were dinosaur bones as well.

If we had kept walking west and a little north, we would have ended up on the ranch where the UFO had crashed only a few years earlier.

I finally got past the trouble with the gun drawer, because the war trophies disappeared, finding their way into my Uncle Bob's collection, where they remain to this day. Some fascinating artifacts, from a time when the entire world was at war. Those things don't just lie quietly in the bottom of a chest somewhere, just as our memories of those times don't vanish. My Uncle Penny decided to go back years later, to make sure he'd seen what he'd seen and reaffirm that his life was still unbroken. Everyone warned him against it, afraid that it would turn out badly for him, but he would hear none of it.

It has crept slowly into my own thinking, sitting as I do safely away from Viet Nam, separated by over thirty years, that I may want to do exactly what my Uncle Penny and my Uncle Bob both did. It's a strange thing that happens, I suppose a built-in trait of human beings, that as you get older, you have to go back to refresh your memory from time to time, to remember and reflect on things that were important and visit old friends who may have been lost along the way.

That became very apparent when I was hoodwinked by my friend Bob Brewin into going up to the Vietnam Memorial in Washington in November of 1982. And it was very real traveling out across the New Mexico desert during the blinding thunderstorm near the Bottomless Lakes. That thunderstorm, like the ones before that got the unsuspecting Sky Riders and poor Jack Valentine, jolted me into a frame of mind unlike any other, rearranging the interior wiring, and propelled me further along on the trail to the Sacred Mountain.

It seemed to open up my mind to the idea that where there is great resistance, there is a great deal of transcendence. Where a lot of energy is expended, there is an equal amount of energy becoming quiet. I saw that in operation when a round zapped the kid at the backside of Tan Son Nhut, and he just lay down over the parapet and ceased to exist. I saw his spirit leave his body, the way someone would get out of a car that was broken and walk away.

If there are strange things happening out on the New Mexico desert around Roswell, it could be because the spirits of the dead strangers on the UFO had no place to go and are still wandering around scaring the livestock and giving rise to spooky stories told by old ranchers over their morning coffee in the truck stop cafes.

I haven't been to the beaches at Normandy or in Italy, but have seen for myself the ravaged wastes of places in Viet Nam and felt the presence of spirits who have been left behind and don't know where they are or where to go. There is a theory that everything that is happening in one place has a perfect duplicate in another, that it is possible to exist on more than one plane at a time. Sometimes memory does that, in a strange way. and our existence seems to fragment and turn in many different directions in the space of a breath.

I was still with my first wife when my Uncle Penny landed on Salerno again. It was different than his first trip through, when the Germans were waiting for the invaders. I was stuck with her and her dad and his far-to-the-right-of-the-John-Birch-Society stand, just as my uncle's unit had been stuck on the beach for a month, barely able to hold onto enough land to avoid being driven back into the sea. They were headquartered in a peasant's farmhouse. The G.I.s got to know the family well and made a Christmas by decorating the barn for the kids that holiday. The oldest son was nine years old, and it seemed as though no one there would live to celebrate New Year's. I remember the small Vietnamese children who lived near the back gate of Tan Son Nhut watching with awe-filled eyes as we set up the small artificial tree with its delicate little Christmas lights. I can still hear their delighted laughter mingled in with the rattle of small-arms fire.

And now they say they are banning fireworks in Viet Nam, for safety reasons.

I like these subtle paradoxes.

Like the Italians as soldiers. They are a wonderful, resilient lot, and if I ever have to go to war again, I will pray for them as my enemies. My Uncle Penny somehow made it through that impossible time trapped on that small strip of beachhead and came home, where he devoted himself to a marriage and kids. Even then, there was a sadness to his life that was like a shadow of the war. His wife and youngest son were killed in a car crash on the Panhandle, on the Running Water Draw. He came into my bedroom one early morning in July 1954 and told me his wife had died in the night. Just walked out, down the hall past the room where my grandfather had kept all the war trophies his number-one son had sent him, and on out the front door. If he could have, he would have walked on into the mirror of another existence. My mind had a difficult time dealing with that then, because we all loved Flossie, the vibrant, slightly wild young woman who would haul us all off on the Santa Fe Chief for a day of shopping at the army surplus store in Amarillo. They said she was speeding the day she crashed, which she probably was, but then again that was the way she greeted life, head-on, and with open arms.

That's a trait I have been trying to learn to act on. Like learning not to shut your eyes when you're handling hardware. Point and squeeeeeezzzzzzeeeeeee.

Never blink. Always keep your eye on the target.

My Uncle Penny blinked and remarried, and it was a few years later when he announced he was going back to Italy to find Babbo, which was what they called the Italian farmer, because they couldn't pronounce his name. I had been stuck on a beachhead just like Salerno while I was with wife number one, and the fighting was just as fierce.

She was a lovely girl and went on to adulthood and child-rearing, I'm sure, without ever having looked back once with

126

regret. Actually, we were very good for each other, for I drove her a little nearer to her awareness of the Road, and she delivered me to my local draft board in Parmer County in 1965. There are big, momentous things that happen in everyone's life, and Cheryl was one of them in mine. Like finding a key to a door that you don't know you're going to go through, but one day, there you are.

She meant well, and so did I. It's that sort of savage innocence that really turns your heart to ice. In Viet Nam I saw it every day, dealing with people who bore you no good will, and even though I couldn't comprehend much of their lingo, I could feel their fear and resentment.

And in some cases, outright hatred.

Like the prisoners we captured on the back perimeter of Tan Son Nhut, who rode in a frozen silence in the back of the deuce-n-half, their half-lidded eyes as deadly as a cobra's. I could feel their rage and knew they were a formidable enemy.

It was confusing to see what they had on them when we were preparing to turn them over to Intelligence. One of them, a very young man with an oozing wound on his arm, had a picture of his wife and baby wrapped carefully in rice paper and inserted into a G.I. baggie to waterproof it. He was also carrying an M-16 rifle, with three bandoliers of fresh ammunition. I tried to hate him, but there was a slight chink in my armor by then. l feared him and knew he would kill me if he had the chance, and knew I would kill him if I was driven to do it. It was at that moment that I got an odd feeling that I was looking at another one of the strange markers that line the Road, angry and relieved at how easily it all falls into place, provided you stay around long enough to see that it is all of a perfect warp and weave.

When it reaches the point of questioning everything, it gets very hard to put a round between someone's running lights, and the Road becomes a lot narrower.

That feeling passed fleetingly away back then, but there was an awareness that stayed with me. Cheryl was a more pragmatic person about those kinds of things, and when I arrived back at the big air base in Seattle one early morning in the belly of a C-141 Starlifter, full of my plans of going to see her, now that I was escaped from the killing fields and ready to get on with my life, I was informed she had run off with a man who owned department stores in the Midwest.

And when we were finally mustered out, and driven to the Seattle/Tacoma airport, we were greeted at almost every turn by protesters who were carrying the flag of North Viet Nam and threw eggs at us. or chanted that we were all baby-killers.

It made for a very strange homecoming. Even though I was back on United States soil, in the state of Washington, I might as well have been on the moon. When my Uncle Penny talked about returning to Italy back then, the war had been over for eighteen years. I wasn't exactly sure of why that moved me so deeply, but it did, and it does so even more now, thinking about my own return to a country which had been at war with us and now is asking for American tourists.

While the bombs and bullets didn't do much for the final victory, Levis and Honda 90s and rock-'n'-roll took their ultimate toll and finally turned the tides of war.

In its aftermath is when you find the real gems and begin to know what it all means. My Uncle Penny believed so strongly in finding old Babbo that he was willing to take his new wife and another couple to tour all the trendy spots in a newly fashionable Europe, if that would let him look for a peasant farmer he had shared living space with for over a month in a time when there were no tomorrows. He found the area where it had happened totally changed. Never giving up, he hired a cab driver to help him track down the family. His wife and their friends went on to sightsee in Venice while he played at his silly detective work. By sheer persistence, they located the farm, but the current residents knew nothing of a man called Babbo or his family. The cabbie was in tears, trying to comfort my uncle on the street, when a man on a motorcycle went by, then stopped suddenly and came back.

"Captain Anderson?" the man called out, unbelievingly.

It was the nine-year-old boy who was now a grown man and remembered that Christmas in the war and the G.I.s who were there.

The reunion was one I can only imagine, knowing what I know now. I've gone totally mushy, and carry Kleenex for those kinds of events, which seem to be becoming more frequent.

Or that I begin to see more often now.

Even my uncle's new wife was moved, deciding that it had been a splendid idea, that instead of simply bouncing around trendy European watering holes, they had done something of importance, which they had. It was a sign as big as a house about the Road and the Journey. Even trapped as I was in the bitter battle that was my marriage, slogging along in inch-by-inch progress, I saw and felt that what happened was more than just an amusing travel story to be told over dinner.

I had become like my Uncle Penny, pinned down on a very dangerous beachhead, unable to go forward or back. And in just the same way, what had been the most daunting of circumstances turned out to have been the exact ingredient to push me forward, past the seemingly overwhelming odds.

There was an old saw that went, "Just when it looks the darkest, it gets totally black," that went around the ranks when I was in Viet Nam, along with the idea that the shorter you became (short meaning short-timer in-country), the better target you made. Those were events that opened some inner door of awareness, and whether recognized or not, were recorded somewhere in the consciousness.

Sometimes the events are large-scale, like the wars that come and go, sometimes it's nothing more than a child's cry, or the beauty of a sunset. It almost always happens at some point on a motorcycle trip, or a voyage on a boat, and probably flying as well.

Just hearing an account of them will do the trick, if a person is accustomed to looking for clues.

Mooch Crane would have called all that a horse-feather, which is something that tickled you, but which you couldn't put your finger on.

"Like planting a crop," he'd say, shifting around in the cab of his pickup. "What kind of man do you think would spend all day long sitting out here on a tractor, acting like he had good sense, and then go down to the bank to borrow money to plant something that might or might not grow?" He'd laugh and take his weather-beaten old work hat off, then pull it back on. "Who'd be the craziest? The farmer or the banker?" That would send him into gulps of his odd laugh, but I've often thought of the horse-feathers that we see every day without giving them much thought.

It's good to ask a few questions once in a while, even if we don't know what we're looking to find out.

And it's good to remember that no matter what tack you're on, you're bound to have a wind shift.

Bertie Einstein said that if you set out in a straight line, you'd come right back to where you started from, if you just stayed with it.

Riding for the buzzer, as Delvin would put it.

Try to hold onto the pick-up man and not get trampled when you have a get-off.

Rodeo philosophy which works in all applications.

The Perfume River

I always thought I'd like to get it up on the Perfume River, maybe about sunset.

Just the name makes it okay to die.

The Perfume River.

Pictures of dark men in hats from the twenties and thirties come to mind, standing with exotic women in front of old Renaults.

The French Foreign Legion was there for a while, and I remember seeing a Frank Sinatra movie about Indo-China somewhere along the way. Nat King Cole sang a great song called "China Gate," and there were a lot of action shots with the old foot-on-the-punji-stake scene, or the primitive but effective bamboo spike snap-back traps laid out in the trackless jungle. John Wayne did "The Green Berets" years later. I got to see that film "in-country." We were all sitting out on the ammo crates at the open-air theater waiting for Stella Stevens in "Waterhole #3," and they gave us "The Green Berets."

I had never seen a crude plywood movie screen ventilated the way that one was, and there was a full alert thrown up all over the compound, because the brass thought we had come under heavy attack. That took some explaining, but Top made it right in the end with a phone call to the commanding general of the brigade, who had served with Top back when he was a green second lieutenant.

The PMO wanted a full report, which we gave him, but it wasn't anything to do with Stella Stevens not showing up, or that the entire audience rose up as one to protest seeing John's movie, they all just happened to be packing their weapons.

It was an effective protest, when all was said and done, and we had no more movies, which was just as well. The VC had discovered a ready-made target on movie nights and had been in the habit of lobbing a mortar round or two into the gathering. It sort of ruined your movie, what with the scattered popcorn and spilled beer.

Charlie was working his way up to a really good show when the cancellation call came down.

He paid us back for that later, when Tet came.

In between 1 was studying the Buddhist monks, watching them as we went about our daily business, as I also watched the beautiful Eurasian girls in lovely silk pants and tops, so wonderfully colorful and mysterious. On one stretch of road, we'd always see the same two monks pushing old Raleigh bicycles to and from their ancient pagoda, which was carved with many different scenes, from elephants to strange monkey gods, rising up all the way to the top of the spire that rose above the ground to a height of almost a hundred feet. When Intelligence discovered that the enemy was using the pagoda as an aiming point to drop in mortar and rocket fire on MAC-V Headquarters, they gave the order to destroy it.

Every day we'd roll by the pagoda, and the two monks would wave to us, and I'd wonder if they were still going to be waving after some piece of our vast arsenal reduced their church to tiny pieces of holy rubble. I marveled at the fact that somehow or other, nothing ever worked, and the pagoda was still standing when I left Viet Nam.

I'd wonder about the various ways you could buy it in a war. I was comfortable with everything but being burned up. Or gut-shot and left to die screaming. A clean round through the running lights or a 122 mm. rocket wouldn't be anything to bitch about.

Nothing. Here one second, gone the next.

Going suddenly like that, though, might lead to some confusion. I've seen evidence of dead guys not knowing they're dead and kind of hanging around, like someone waiting for a date who's late, or being first in line for tickets to a Rolling

Stones concert. There were some places in our area of operation where there were French ghost soldiers still lingering on, bringing an almost overwhelming sense of sadness and loss, and hopelessness. We had the Buddhist monks do a cleansing ceremony one afternoon, and after another few days the spirits were gone. In the frame of mind I was in then, I don't know if I believed the business about someone being hung-fire in the hallway between planes, but there was a sensation of someone or something being there before, which left me feeling depressed and sad when I was around too long.

After the two monks came and walked around with their incense and prayers, it lightened up.

They were the same two monks Roess pointed out later, saying that as long as we saw them, everything was all right.

Tiger and Foo said there were strangers sometimes in the French Cemetery and around the Phu Tho Racetrack, which turned out to be the VC and NVA, who had begun building up their positions there. I found out later both the Coke boys saw the spirits of the dead, only they didn't relate to them that way.

I thought anyone who could invent something like Pernod would be the sort who would haunt places with a vengeance. Believing as I did in some sort of poetic justice, and sharing Bertie Camus's sense of the absurd, I especially liked the idea of French-speaking ghosts lingering in the French Cemetery, where the NVA and VC had dug an elaborate maze of tunnels and even set up a field hospital to treat their wounded.

The French Cemetery and the Phu Tho Racetrack were still not under our control when I left country in August 1968.

Saigon was "the Paris of the Orient," and you could wander down one of the wide, tree-lined boulevards and hear a dozen languages spoken. You could also end up with an AK-47 round through your gizzard, or a hand grenade dumped in your jeep gas tank, which was a favorite for the unwary driver in the dense traffic. The filler holes were large, and a rubber band around the spoon of the grenade might hold together for some time.

133

When it let go, you have never seen such spectacular fireworks.

Crude, but very effective.

Sergeant Posey, our motor pool sergeant, put a grate in the filler necks of our vehicles, which was such an innovation that a motor officer from San Francisco flew over to interview him and study his design to see whether or not it was needed on all U.S. vehicles that were operating in the war zone.

If Sergeant Posey had been around with Arkin years later, he probably would have come up with a device to keep a hose from being placed in the exhaust, or prevent you from starting the car in an enclosed space. Arkin talked of suicide during those first few months I knew him, but I thought that was all by the boards. Kid Chocolate might get hammered in the ring, but he would never give in. Pure heart would keep him on his feet, no matter what sort of punishment was dealt out.

He hadn't heard about the Roswell crash, and I never thought to tell him.

Or it had slipped my mind just like it had with Arty. Things like that are hard to hold onto, and they drift in and out of reality sometimes. Standing by the APC (armored personnel carrier) watching the changing scenes of Saigon, I felt I had been thrown into a river of humanity swirling unendingly about me, and it made it hard to concentrate on odd truths, like the strange lights we'd see when we were visiting the guard towers or lying flat on our backs outside the runways at Tan Son Nhut, watching the Phantoms take off for bombing runs off to the north of the city. Some nights we'd see enough of them to make us think we'd found another Milky Way. On other nights there would only be one or two.

When I asked Foo about the lights, he shrugged his small shoulders and smiled. "Maybe our grandfather looking for his way. They come all the time. We call them grandfather lamps."

I could never get either of the Coke boys to explain themselves any further. If I pressed too hard, they said it was G.I. airplanes.

I'd always kind of hoped it would be one of the motherships coming back, maybe to straighten out the whole mess, but there wasn't any luck with that.

After the experience with the French ghosts, I never really knew what to make of much of anything. The pretty whore who worked the Rialto Tea House said she could make you see the Jade Temple when she made love to you, but even she was afraid to talk about the spirits around the French Cemetery, or the bright little lights that moved about in the skies above the room where she worked. mingling with the stars.

It wouldn't be quite the same, getting it in a "bone orchard."

Not like catching one up on the Perfume River. I've wondered about my friend Arkin, parked in a Honda sedan with a hose from the exhaust into the passenger side window, and Ernest Hemingway, sucking on a 12 gauge in his kitchen up in Ketchum, Idaho. It might have been all right to lose your Slip Shift and disappear into a Kansas sky and never be heard from again, or maybe topping out a hill somewhere in the mountains of New Mexico at about a hundred and seeing how far you could make the bike fly.

It wouldn't carry the same weight as being stung by one of those little lead bees up on the Perfume River. If there is anything to this whole idea of closures, then I'll be standing around somewhere one day, and that spent round that's been waiting all this time will finally find me.

We all have our time marked. The chaos of the universe is orderly, to say the least, and there is something of relief knowing that once you claim your death, you're free of it.

Charlie Norton's words always come back to me when I'm through his old neck of the woods. "You just wake up one morning in another line shack, riding for another brand."

There's something to be said for Charlie's working cowboy approach.

A Sane Man in the Keys

I got to Coconut Grove a day late and a dollar short.

Like the bohemian movement and the beatniks, the time span for the happening in Coconut Grove was long enough for me to read about and dream about, but by the time I arrived, it was mostly filled with a lot of people hanging around and waiting for something to happen.

Like going into Sloppy Joe's in Key West, thinking you'd pick up a leftover muse from Ernest Hemingway. I did manage to see his house there before they turned it into a hands-off affair that you had to stand carefully back from, when there were still descendants of his famous six-toed cat Boise. When I went through the joint in 1976, there were cats enough for everyone. You could carry one around with you, if you wanted, while you looked at where Ernie worked on *To Have and Have Not*. There was a breeze coming off the Gulf the day I was there, and you could smell Cuba, not like the stench off the mess it is now, but back when it was still Cuba and there was some romance left about Castro. I thought about running away and joining his revolution when I was young. Who knows, maybe I should have. That's what makes life worth living, not having great regrets. It seems you get more points for doing more things, even if some of them turn out to be not such hot ideas.

One hot idea I had and always liked was that trip down to Key West to see Hemingway's joint. It occurred to me then that I'd need to take a luck-piece to leave on Ernie's grave up in Ketchum, Idaho.

It was on that same trip that I stopped off at one of the other keys to look over a fishing camp and came across Gordon. No last name, because he's not the type who'd want publicity, and also because of his kid deserving a fighting chance of staying afloat.

Gordon's son was born with an IQ of about 50, and the doctors said it would be best if he were confined to a hospital. Tough on the mom and dad, but best for society as a whole. Gordon was an unusual man, and he decided that what needed to be done was to find his son a companion with about the same IQ and try to teach them both a few tricks of the trade, like how to brush your teeth, use the bathroom, eat at table, maybe even work a little among your peers.

What Gordon came up with was a chimpanzee.

They lived together in the fishing camp on the keys, and the kid and the chimp both thrived. I thought back on my own childhood and wondered how we all might have turned out if we had had that kind of gentle loving-kindness shown us. I wasn't much of a fisherman, but I liked going out with a pole and sitting in the boat staring off at the Gulf, watching the same wind and waves that Hemingway saw every day back when. There's something to walking around in big cathedrals that turns your mind to try to find echoes of some great man's passage. I remember standing in the Tower of London hearing the faint murmurs of history clamoring with one another, listening to Willy Shakespeare try to sort it all out. I felt the same thing at the old pagoda in Viet Nam, watching the two Buddhist monks at their prayers. Times like that, you keep looking over your shoulder to see who's watching.

Sitting in Gordon's fish-camp on the Keys was another sort of deal, more immediate in dredging up reactions. He was a funny man, and married to a beautiful, funny woman. Their other son was a healthy, bright boy who thought his brother was special.

It meant they both got to live with a chimp.

That might have been the way my friend Pat Boatwright grew up, because he wound up diving for NASA to retrieve space capsules back when they started the Mercury program.

137

He was more porpoise than human. He came from Florida and started his long and colorful career right there in Coconut Grove, and he was probably responsible for a lot of the stories I had heard that made me want to move there.

One of my favorites was the stolen Bertram sport-fisherman, with a big tuna-tower on it so you could spot the big ones when you were out in the Stream. Pat had had more than a few and for some reason decided he wanted to go see an old girlfriend on one of the small islands in the Bahamas. Needing a boat, he got on the first one that came to hand. It was in at the gas dock of a big marina, taking on fuel. The skipper had evidently stepped ashore to pay when Pat went aboard and cast off.

His excuse was that the girl was very pretty.

The River Police chased him up and down Miami causeways until he finally took off the tuna-tower under a bridge. When they hauled him into the station, the irate desk sergeant demanded to know what his occupation was.

"Gunfighter," replied Pat, irate right back.

I tried that line not long after I'd heard it when they'd hauled me into The Fort on St. Thomas. It was not a nice place to be jailed. When the very angry desk sergeant asked my occupation, I replied, "Gunfighter," just like Pat. When they started to book me, I changed my tune and plead "otter." I insisted I'd said otter.

Occupation otter. A good thing to be. My friend Bear was Bear, and I went by, and still do, the name Otter. It appeals to my sense of oneness with nature, and if I press my magic wrist, I do turn into a playful, cute river otter. It was one of the things that don't come along right away, that you have to sneak up on. Like what would you say if you came upon one of the Sky Riders who'd crashed outside Roswell.

Mr. Isadore would have launched right in on them, and probably would have asked if they had any way of seeing into the past. He was always very interested in what had really happened to *La Trumpuse*, and he was intrigued with the idea that there was a German U-boat lost somewhere in the area.

Marcel, the French skipper who had brought the *Marcel B.* across from Gibraltar, had told him that story, and it was a splinter in Mr. Isadore's saddle blanket until the day he died.

There was a rumor that the U-boat carried a chart aboard marking the location of one of the Holy Libraries. That was the other thing Mr. Isadore was into. He said there were four, and one of them was out in the area known as the Bermuda Triangle. The mysterious force there was in place to protect the Holy Library. He said the porpoises there were ancient Atlanteans who had changed their forms and stayed on to guard the knowledge of the temple, making sure no one could take the secrets there and use them for their own selfish gain.

Marcel told Mr. Isadore that Hitler got wind of the existence of the libraries and devised a plan for one of his U-boats to locate it and bring its contents to him. Just like the oil reserves that were supposed to be in the vast fields in the center of the earth. Hitler talked to a lot of psychics and seers, and some of them had good information, but there wasn't anyone to explain how you would carry out a scheme to find them. Lionel Ledbetter searched all over Palo Duro Canyon for the opening to the great underground river, but it is still hidden. Maybe Richard Perry stumbled across one of those entrances to the center of the earth on that last long ramble across the frozen wastes of the Arctic, but he carried his secret to the grave. Mooch Crane knew about slip shifts, and changing planes that way, and about the wreckage of the UFO in Roswell, but he never said much about it. Pat Boatwright knew about the U-boat but said it was better left alone. His friend and diving partner Cookie said he would never dive on a ghost-boat. To get the chart, you'd have to go into the tomb of the sailors on the sub to retrieve it.

Pat told me later he had actually seen the U-boat when they were doing a salvage dive not far from his girlfriend's island in the Bahamas. The locals knew about it but never said anything because of the bad luck it would cause. They said there had already been crews trying to bring it up and make a circus of it, charging admission and selling the remains of the crew back to Germany. A blow came through not long after the operation started, and three people were drowned, and equipment failures finished the act.

Charlie Norton knew the whereabouts of Spanish gold hidden up in the desert mountains where he ran his cattle in Chihuahua, but it belonged to the dead. Just like the monster cave his friend had found. Thinking about Lionel, I wonder if that sinkhole Elkins stumbled onto wasn't really an entrance to the very thing everyone was searching for, a path to Middle Earth.

So Gordon got a chimp to come live with his family in the Keys, and Boatwright steered clear of the U-boat with the chart for the Holy Libraries. Some things only remain true so long as you know the truth of them is in your heart. Finding the gold stash, and taking away a simple fossil as your prize, like Charlie Norton. He showed me the chambered nautilus he found on the site, kept it over his mantel.

"All this country was under water one time, and this feller here was making a living off the same place my stock are now." He rolled a cigarette with one hand, smiling that leather-wrinkled smile. "Only now it just ain't as wet."

A chimp can brush his teeth, pass the potatoes, tie his shoes, and give you a hug as big as Dallas. He's covered with fur, and can't talk plain lingo, but he can pass on the simple gifts of life that make this business all worthwhile ever so often, and they remember who their friends are.

A Bear at Duffy's Place in the Sun

The Spanish Main has always been a draw in lore and legend, and a lot of it has to do with the kinds of colorful characters that are drawn to places like Charlotte Amalie, or Jost Van Dyke, or Road Town. The Caribbean covers land that used to be above water, where Atlantis supposedly went down. Or what one would describe as Atlantis. It was a lot bigger than what the old classical writers have described as the island, and it was much older as well. The Bermuda Triangle is nothing more than what might be described as a doormat for that part of the world. My good friend and sailing partner Duncan McGregor told me his theory, which was that anyone lucky enough to see a whale in the water would be taken to a next higher level of existence without question. After watching a forty-foot animal cruise by us in the middle of the night, I began to see his point. The evening it happened, I looked over the starboard rail, and there he was, a being in a body longer than the boat I was on. When I called below, Duncan told me he probably wanted to listen to some music on the radio, which he proceeded to turn on.

The big guy beside us rolled on alongside for a while, until he got tired of the music, or had other pressing appointments. Then he just disappeared in a halo of moonlit bubbles.

Duncan said that often happened to him when he was at sea, and it was quite a lot of company to keep on some nights. Part of it, he said, was that you needed to observe their own whale manners, and if you knew how to do that, you had nothing to worry about.

That was a rule of thumb that could be applied to everything.

If you knew the rules, you'd be all right. Hairspray Tom didn't know the rules, or knew them and couldn't or wouldn't follow them. He was in the habit of being thrown down the steps from the Crow's Nest, or from Duffy's joint, for urinating on the dance floor or standing at the bar taking a whizz while he guzzled someone else's drink. On Wednesdays, Pat Boatwright had a freebie hour when he handed out lobster and beer, which would have made him the most popular bar on the waterfront, except for the fact that all the rummies and freeloaders on the island found out about it and were waiting in line. No tourists off the cruise ships in the harbor could worm their way through that motley-looking crew, so that wonderful idea went the way of the old wooden docks at Yacht Haven Marina when the Sheraton chain bought it out and hired Nevada and Pat to dispose of the old pilings.

Roger Nicely was Nevada's real name, and he'd earned it in the mines of the state he was named after. It was said he could shave you with nitro and never leave a nick. That is if he was sober. Drunk, you never knew what might happen.

Like when he kept getting his Volkswagen stolen from the Yacht Haven parking lot. Three times of breaking that sacred rule about leaving one's car alone was too much for Nevada, so he rigged up a VW as bait, with a shaped charge under the driver's seat that when the thief hot-wired it and tried to drive off would send him up through the top of the car, and it didn't have a sunroof.

Nevada's big mistake was coming into the bar and laughing to himself until someone asked him what was so funny.

"Go boom," he replied, and fell into another fit of gruff laughter. "I'm waiting for the boom."

There was an off-duty policeman drinking at the bar that night, and he asked what he meant by that, and Nevada told him, which upset the officer quite a lot. He went down with Nevada and watched while he disarmed it, although it turned out that not all of the bomb was taken out of the car. What was left was only to scare someone, which it did later on that night when Nevada got into it to drive home, too drunk to remember he'd rigged it with explosives meant for a thief.

We took up a collection and bought the policeman another round for saving our friend from himself. No one had forgotten the tremendous fireworks that Nevada and Pat had given Charlotte Amalie by overcharging the wooden pilings that held up the old Yacht Haven Marina. Pieces of wood and concrete showered the entire harbor area when that bit of work went up. It damaged cruise ships and sank a forty-five-foot Bertram from Puerto Rico out in the harbor, leaving nothing showing of it but the tuna tower.

The boys stayed gone for a month or so, until the big shots from the Sheraton Corporation cooled down. Mrs. Rabbit was having an afternoon party on her veranda the day the marina went up. She said it was like the first day of the shelling of the small village where she and Mr. Rabbit had been living when the Japanese went into Manchuria.

It was difficult to get around Mrs. Rabbit, but Pat convinced her in the end that it was a flaw in the dynamite they were using, and she bought the story. Pat and Nevada were off the hook when it was announced in the *Daily News* of St. Thomas that there would be a cocktail party honoring the two bad boys, given by Mrs. Gertrude Rabbit.

Those in the know in the Sheraton hotel chain made it a rule of thumb to never go against the grand old island lady, and even the governor attended the affair. It was as though life in the islands was affected greatly by being situated directly on one of the great Dragon Lines that crisscross the known world.

No such luck for Hairspray Tom or Hopsack Harry, though, two pathetic drunks who hung out at Pat's bar above Duffy's Place in the Sun nightclub. I was prone to coming to in front of the Gonzolo Market from time to time after a night of too many spirits, and there would be Hairspray and Hopsack, full of their sad stories to coax drinking money out of the seersucker-clad tourists from the cruise boats, on their way to breakfast at the Normandy or Escargot. I had my own room at Duffy's so I would rise and shine and go to it, where I would have to explain to the manager, a great bear of a man named Ken Hawk, how it was I had fallen asleep at the market with the common drunks who were ruining Pat and his Wednesday freebie nights.

It was at Pat's where Scott McKenzie started singing, and we did the poetry wall, and met Johnny the Tenor. The Crow's Nest was well know even before Pat and Nevada dredged three feet off the harbor bottom. A Navy Seal team out of Puerto Rico who regularly made the liquor run for the naval base there came there for R&R. I got along well with one of the guys, who had a trick of hollering out, "Incoming!" and toppling backwards off the rail he was sitting on, landing deftly on his feet in the alley below. That caused quite a flap at the bar one Wednesday afternoon, when a dozen German tourists somehow wandered up. When the elderly lady in pearls saw the Seal go over, she dropped like a rock. The quick thinking of the Seals and the FMS team saved her, but the acting police chief asked my friend Mr. Shulterbrandt to please have a talk with Pat about his patrons. Mr. Shulterbrandt didn't have to, for Mrs. Rabbit heard about the affair and spent all of an hour with Pat at a back table in earnest conversation.

When I asked him about it later, his reply was that he would rather swim naked with sharks than be chewed out by Mrs. Rabbit again.

Another rule of thumb outlined, to be observed at all cost.

She invited the Seal team from Puerto Rico over to one of her famous afternoon cocktail parties. To everyone's surprise, the boys were perfect gentlemen, and they ended up making her the mascot for their unit.

It was not unusual afterwards to see the big PT-type Seal boat docked at Mrs. Rabbit's on Wednesdays.

I know well what Pat was talking about, for I had had my time before the mast with the grand old lady, who was convinced that if Mr. Rabbit had just been alive, everything would have been all right, for he would have had a heart-to-heart with me.

144

Just being on her wrong side was bad enough.

After my session with her, I would have just as soon have been beaten by goons as face her disapproval again. She got you with those piercing clear blue eyes, saying how disappointed she was in your behavior, that she had had such high expectations of you.

She would have been the one to send to talk to the boys off the UFO outside Roswell. She never made a point of talking about the Road, or the Sacred Mountain, but she didn't have to.

Watching her feed the sea iguanas at Rabbit Point was enough to convince you she was in direct daily contact with the Cosmos, and if you were lucky, just being around her enough would somehow rub off on you. Top Shunk had that effect on us in a war zone. You knew if you were with him, there wasn't a round made that would have your name on it. It was a distorted perception of the truth, but it worked just as well, and it had an after-effect as powerful as the lingering gagging sensation you get when chugging down a straight tequila.

Jacques Cousteau was in port aboard *Calypso* quite a lot during those times, and Mrs. Rabbit was always invited to the shipboard parties. They were very popular affairs, and it was hard to get an invitation. My friend Carter would manage to have a press badge or two left over, so I got to attend a few of the better ones.

There was a mystique concerning the boat and her skipper, and I got to meet the older son Philippe, who was to take over the throne from his father. I don't think the senior Cousteau ever got over the death of his son in the freak flying accident a few years later, and the news of that death was devastating to the rest of the world as well. I had always assumed that there would be someone to carry on his father's work, and never thought I'd see a day arrive where there was little or no recognition of that sea pioneer and his delightful ship and crew.

It was at one of those parties that a guest said something to the effect that the young man probably got exactly what he deserved for going around disturbing all the sea life in the name of science.

Mrs. Rabbit reminded him of that rule of thumb that said to be polite and was told where to put her suggestion. Bear was standing next to her and heard the man's remark, both about Cousteau and to Mrs. Rabbit. Without thinking, he reverted to his bar-clearing tactic of hugging the man to his great paunch, quick-stepped him to the rail of *Calypso*, and heaved him over. It was a grand gesture, accompanied by a strangled screech as the man hit the water, which got the attention of one of the Seals manning their vessel next to the research ship. He dived in and rescued the drowning guest, and hauled the man ashore onto the small island in the middle of the harbor, where he was left wringing wet, shouting at the top of his lungs that he was suing everyone concerned.

There was just the small matter of being able to get back to the harbor front from where he stood dripping on the rocky beach. We found out he spent the rest of the evening there. Only at dawn the next day did a fisherman from Frenchtown ferry him across to the waterfront.

Meanwhile Mrs. Rabbit had a long heart-to-heart with Bear, who was doing his best to evoke some sympathy from her.

"He was a mannerless man, and vexing, but he didn't deserve to just be chucked into the harbor. Why, the wretched fellow might have drowned."

"Oh no, ma'am," explained Bear. "I wouldn't have let him drown."

"And that nice young man from the Seals! I'll have to have them all back over next week. I think I'll throw a party for them, poor dears."

Bear, thinking he was off the hook, started to walk away.

"Young man, you get yourself right back here. I won't let you off so easy. Now you come and sit right there, and see to it that I don't get bothered by any more of that sort of boor."

She quizzed him about what he did, and how he ever got

to the islands, and ended by declaring that she was coming to Duffy's the next evening, since she had never been to a nightclub like that in Charlotte Amalie. She made Bear pick her up in a taxi and give her the full treatment, from dinner at Escargot to midnight dancing at the club. Hairspray Tom and Hopsack Harry were there, but they were playing by the rules most of the night. Both men even danced a short dance with her, when the jukebox was plugged in during the band's breaks.

"Nice young men," she told Bear. "They just need some positive direction."

Bear was obliged to follow her advice until Mrs. Rabbit was gone and the pair reverted to their old ways. Their positive direction in that case was down the stairs again, bumping along over the stone steps.

When Bear and the rest of the club crew went for breakfast at the Gate, he told me he was thinking about going back to teaching in Arizona.

Mrs. Rabbit had gotten to him in that charming-old-lady way she had. I can't recall her speeches, but they were never really threatening, more like the tweaks of guilt my grandmother would use to get me to do something she wanted me to do, for my own good.

What's astounding is how far a human being will go to avoid something like that, ignoring the daily signs that we are in flux, that great forces are at work even now, preparing us for the next level of existence.

It was a funny apprenticeship for recognizing the front porch step that puts you on the Road, but it was effective.

Man is probably the only animal in the world that will go to such great lengths to self-destruct, even standing on the threshold of such incredible discoveries as finding clues to the Road which leads Home.

Charlie Norton used to break his own horses up into his eighties by tying them to the back of his pickup and running them for a mile or so. I like to think of myself hooked up to the back of the Great Spirit's pickup, and dragged along kicking and screaming into a happy destiny.

The other lesson I learned from Hopsack and Hairspray is that after you're thrown down the stairs of Duffy's enough, you begin to think greater things, like being eighty-sixed from saloons on the ground floor.

Simple revelations that are worth the wait.

The Wake of the Edmund Fitzgerald

I was living in Round Pond on the coast of Maine in 1976 when I heard Gordon Lightfoot sing his haunting song about the ore boat lost on Lake Ontario in a November gale. Ian Tyson had introduced me to Lightfoot back in the late sixties at the Tropicana Motel in L.A., where they were both staying. In those days, the Tropicana was the address to have, just down the street from the Troubadour, only a few blocks walk up to Barney's Beanery on the Strip. From there, it was a mere crawl to reach the Rain Check, where the Mod Squad hung out. Maude Tyson said Gordon was one to watch, and it was apparent as I listened to the song that she had been right.

It was a haunting melody that took me back to L.A. in some very troubling times of midnight freeway fights in the car with Scott, long drinking binges with blackouts, and bushwhacked friendships left in the lee of a fast-running catastrophe that was in vogue during those years of the late sixties and early seventies. That was around the time I first ran across Mrs. Rabbit, well before I had put two and two together about the Sky Riders who had crashed in the desert outside Roswell, although it was fairly apparent that the UFOs had been landing for a long time in Southern California.

Joshua Tree was full of believers. I never attended one of the conventions out there, but I probably would have been able to find out information about the Roswell incident.

As though it could have been made any plainer to me than it already was.

It is said that when space objects break through the Earth's atmosphere, it creates a lot of static disturbance in the Force Field, and that's what brings all the outbreaks of unknown diseases and natural disasters, plus the human conflicts that flare up from time to time. Looking at a seemingly endless round of bad storms and long-dormant volcanoes going off unexpectedly, it all falls into place.

People seem to be a lot like those volcanoes. Sit around stewing silently forever, and then one day it's like Etna, and it's had enough.

Goodbye city, goodbye folks.

Like an ARCLIGHT strike in Viet Nam, only bigger, and with a lot more punch.

I listened in on a radio operator calling for one of those strikes one night shortly after the beginning of Tet of '68. Excited kid—there was some big-time lead-slinging going on in his sector. The man who answered might well have been a college dean taking an application for enrollment.

The aftermath was total destruction. Even six miles away, sitting in one of the steel guard towers outside Westmoreland's MAC-V compound, where we had gone to witness the event, I was tossed around violently as the ground rolled and shook under the tremendous pounding from the B-52s.

I knew exactly why they described those strikes as sounding like rolling thunder.

A November gale on the Great Lakes doesn't sound like much if you're sitting snug in a room sipping hot tea and watching the trees blowing around in the wind out your front window. Thinking about a volcano going off loses a little juice when you're reading about it in *National Geographic*, looking at the quaint, crispy critters in the wonderful photographs.

ARCLIGHT is an odd-looking code-word meaning the world is going to fall in on your head, and you won't have any idea where it came from. Not on the scale of volcanoes or gales, but impressive all the same, and can be had for the asking.

Sitting in Barney's Beanery one late November night, not long after Ian Tyson played the Troubadour, I experienced a similar event when I was talking with Eva, the Angel of Barney's, and heard a song on the jukebox. It was the same scraggly kid I had crossed trails with years before in the Village, Bob Dylan, singing "Lay, Lady, Lay."

I could feel the deck pitching, like an ore boat on Lake Ontario. Violent eruptions shook my barstool, but I made a mistake common to me back then and thought what I was feeling was a deep and abiding love of the girl sitting beside me. Another song popular in those volatile times had a line that went, "If you can't be with the one you love, love the one you're with."

I could have saved myself the grief, for the lady only had eyes for my good friend Scott, who was cutting an album with A&M Records called *Stained Glass Morning.* Red the cat was Eva's, and he wrought a little vengeance on Scott for me by scratching him while he was trying to get into bed with his mistress. Willy the Whale, the barkeep, tried to cheer me up, but life was on a skid, and I couldn't grasp the small brass ring. It was like I was caught up in the wake of every single momentous event, from the UFO crash in New Mexico, to wandering over the same ground Lionel was searching out on the Palo Duro, to watching the ARCLIGHT strike from the steel tower at MAC-V, or standing in the knee-high rubble of what was left of a lot of Cholon after Tet of '68, watching the gray smoke cover the sun and wondering if any of us would live through the day. I was sailing along on a tack that crossed trails with important events, which were viewed as through a pair of binoculars turned around. Objects were distant, although they were actually close-up. I could feel the tug of something inside, and I knew it was big, but when you're in the heat of it, you don't have time to stop and do anything much but reload.

When the events surrounding you are larger than life, they cannot be comprehended in a single gulp.

Bangers and mash, that British dish, would be just what the doctor ordered, if one were being sent home to digest all the doings of the world one doesn't quite understand. That, or standing outside Carlsbad, New Mexico, looking out over a lowering sunset sky, just happening to be there when the rescue ship for the Sky Riders finally shows up and the crew wants to go somewhere for coffee, or wondering where exactly it was that Elkins stumbled off into the sinkhole that led to Middle Earth. It didn't seem to do him much good, ending up dead as he did on one of those endless strings of islands out in the Pacific in World War II, but maybe in the Chinese Five-Sided Mirror version of it, something changed up for him in those last few moments that made sense of it all for him.

When I saw the kid from Illinois lie down over the sandbags with that surprised look and that sudden change in his eyes as he watched his life slip away, I knew there was something of that there. Maybe the sailors on the *Edmund Fitzgerald* had it too, just before she rolled over and slid silently into her cold, wet grave.

There's one way of looking at it all, like the poem "The Ball Turret Gunner," wherein the man is washed out of the ball turret with a hose. What do you think of your blue-eyed boy now, Mr. Death, they asked when Buffalo Bill went deep six.

What is it in the voice of Janis Joplin that still stirs the soul, making you uneasy down in that part of you that knows about the UFO outside Roswell and knew all along that the time would come that some effort would have to be made toward the Road. The sea bag would have to be packed and ready, and some early morning down the line, it would start.

"Windshield wipers slapping time, we sung up all the songs that driver knew," Janis sang in "Me and Bobby McGee." I knew it when she was singing in the Sand Box with Scott and I sat listening on my stool stewed to the gills. That part of me that knows truth knew it. I touched the same something of the Cosmos that night that I had seen fleeting shadows of in the war, not willingly or for long, but enough that when I was a bit further down the road, it reached out and pulled my consciousness up a notch or two toward the Bigger Picture.

Jay and Moby the dog knew some things about it out on the

ranch in Tujunga, just over the hill from where they rounded up the Charles Manson family. Jay, sitting in his VW camper feeding Moby, would hold forth on a lot of subjects when he camped on our property, trying to lay low from the law. He supported himself nicely by dealing in high-grade grass to an upscale clientele among the musicians in Laurel Canyon. When the heat was on too much, he would "come to the country," as he put it, where Moby could roam up and down the river and chase sticks until he was unable to walk another step.

Moby was trained to deliver the baggies of grass to each address where Jay had a customer. If Jay didn't like the looks of the street or thought something was out of order, he'd give the command, and Moby would disappear, waiting until he was called. Jay had been in business for a long time and never had been busted for dealing. There was no way to make Moby talk, even if they roughed him up. Tim Hardin was always trying to buy the dog, but animals are loyal beings and stick with their masters through even the toughest of times.

Tim didn't have that luck and didn't outlast his song about the Lady from Baltimore. Another name to add to the list of those who went by the boards, their pale faces vanishing slowly into the wake.

I wonder about Jay and Moby whenever I see an old VW Campmobile. Are they up in Montana or British Columbia panning for gold? Gone to Texas? Moby would be twenty-eight or twenty-nine now.

Old for a dog, but not for a pal.

They played a part in picking up the Trail, in their own way. Benny M., a border prophet, once told me you could serve the Big Amigo by teaching a man to pray, or just as readily by putting a pistol in his ear. Either way, you drive him a little closer to a Higher Power.

I like the economy of that.

Looking out over this storm-tossed existence we're tracking through, I can see the long, white wake of the old *Edmund*

Fitzgerald ahead of us, steaming on toward the country of the Sacred Mountain.

Sitting on that barstool at Barney's Beanery seems like only yesterday, and I hear that Dylan song often, as if to remind me.

What we make of this is what happens next.

Or at least gives us time to pick up our wounded and reload.

The Yellow Wagon With Green Wheels

One of the prescriptions for sanity my friend Carter always recommended was *The Wind in the Willows*. It never seems to grow old, and no matter how old you've grown yourself, it is timely and to the point. Pick up the book and turn to any page, and there will immediately be something you'd forgotten about, and the next thing you know, you're hooked.

Those are the things in life that you know you can count on when there's ten of them at the door and your gun's jammed.

Little bits of information that help ease the pain of the road when you're on what the Aborigines of Australia call a walkabout.

Just another way of saying the Road to the Sacred Mountain.

I've always thought it odd that the information we need is the simplest there is, yet the hardest to find. I can get an exact how-to-do-it manual on my Volkswagen Jetta, but there aren't any instructions like that available about how to do this business of living and figuring out what it's all about.

Jim Poteet, moto-genius and observer of life from the ancient Hippie Nation, wisely notes that what you really want to do is stay out of a tank-slapper.

That's a description that concerns motorcycles and a speed wobble. It snatches the bars out of your hands and rapidly moves back and forth in a motion that hits bar ends on both sides of the tank. It is a situation no one ever wants to be in. Once experienced, it is never forgotten.

I would rate it up there with watching the tank-slapper the Sky Riders had when they bought it outside Roswell. Even UFOs have flaws.

I don't know if Kenneth Grahame ever had a tank-slapper or saw Sky Riders. He was a fellow who lived in England quite a few years ago and observed life on the River Thames near his home in Pangbourne. If he had lived in Roswell, he would have written the same sort of book, only it would have had coyotes and rattlesnakes and bobcats as the characters. Charlie Norton never read the book—he *was* the book, without knowing it. Badger fitted Charlie well, gruff and brusque as he was, but kindly and patient, if you had the good sense to call him sir and ask plenty of questions.

The first times I read *The Wind in the Willows*, I was already older and aware that it was more than a children's book. Great things can be read at that level, and it will mean as much to a six-year-old as it does to a grown adult. I was home on leave, getting ready to report to the Oakland Replacement Depot, and I holed up with the book one long afternoon and took my friend Carter's advice.

I had already stumbled across *The Lord of the Rings* and had hoped to run into hobbits somewhere along the way, but I wasn't having much luck. The mother ship had put us down and left us to the mercy of those dead souls who have deserts for hearts.

That's the other plight of the person who one day wakes up and realizes that there's more to it all than just growing up and becoming a big person, buying houses and cars along the way, and raising families. All that's a part of it, but somewhere along the line, the important information got deleted.

It usually takes something like lying in a faded room in a rental house, usually an off-shade of green, waiting for the ax to fall. I had orders in my bag, and an airline ticket, and the bus was rolling. I was on it whether I wanted to be or not. It usually happens that way. You just look up, and there you are.

My old pal Arty Newingham, who perished from the war and the aftermath of Viet Nam, was always looking around with those big innocent eyes and asking, "Where's the door?"

A good question, in the worst of times.

No one told Arty about *The Wind in the Willows*, and it all caught up with him in Moline, Illinois, sometime in 1969. My call was a month too late. He was the first of many friends who were killed by the war but didn't die until later, back in The World.

See you next time.

The Road still beckons, and whether you're riding in Toad's motorcar or walking, it all goes the same direction. The trick is to find out that there is a direction.

"Where's the door?" is still a good question when you're considering everything from the middle of the gunplay.

The phone call I made to Moline was answered by Arty's father. It was one of the worst moments I can remember, hearing him break down and sob when I said who I was and wanted to know how my pal was doing. Those are times like mortal wounds—you come out of the coma just long enough to suffer a little more before you go.

Or coming out of a drunken blackout to find you've just killed someone in a car wreck. There are things in this life that are worse than just dying.

Looking around at the world from inside the stainless-steel ball bearing I was living in then, it was pretty grim. I got grateful later for being able to have that protection, for there was nothing else much to take away the pain.

Pounded by the Cosmic Two-by-Four.

It might come in some spectacular fashion, like sitting in a lunar lander on the face of the moon, wondering if it's going to light back off, or it might be years of getting up and going to work at the factory, trying to feed the kids and keep the mortgage paid.

There does come a day, though, when you walk out the front door, and you see hobbit tracks and think thoughts of a walkabout or just decide to set out in the yellow wagon with the green wheels.

Charlie Norton told me about a friend of his back in the old days who just upped and decided to ride west. No outside reason for it, he just got "itchy feet." Charlie didn't hear from him for months, until he rode back into Chihuahua while Charlie was branding. Never said a word about where he'd been until they were having a beer one night at Al Rivera's place weeks later.

Charlie finally asked him where he'd been straight out, and the reply was a short one.

"Ridin'."

The man was dead by the time I met Charlie so I never got a chance to talk to him, although I suspect I would have heard a familiar tale, if he'd had a mind to jaw a little.

A lot of people have seen hobbit tracks and don't yap about it. They just set off and go, like Charlie's friend. A lot of people have seen them but don't know what they are yet.

Charlie told me about the tinhorn who'd moved out to that neck of the woods and came by one afternoon trying to get help tracking a pack of coyotes that had gotten one of his calves.

"I could tell by lookin' at his new saddle gun we'd be in for a long winter," related Charlie, shaking his head and rolling a cigarette. "It was a 94 Model Winchester, and it ain't never been shot," he went on. "He'd be waitin' for a damn coyote out there in the dark, and first thing he'd hear, he'd squeeze one off. Hell, we lost more damn cattle to that little pipsqueak than we ever did to the coyotes."

Part of the trick of being a successful hunter is knowing what you've got in your gun sights. My grandfather taught me that as a pup, and Charlie Norton was talking about it years later.

Charlie also talked about diplomacy. He'd been known to feed the coyotes on the land where he ran his cattle.

There are few mistakes more costly than those that kick the chair out from under you when you've got a noose around your neck.

Eliminate those, and your life has fewer potholes and deep ditches to fall into.

My friend Flobird always said everyone recognizes them, sooner or later.

She and Charlie would have been a pair, but the universe is a big backyard to play in, and they never crossed trails, except that they moved into the big time at about the same instant in this split second we call life.

They had both been on the Road in the yellow wagon with the green wheels, and their report was pretty much the same as what Kenneth Grahame said about it in his book.

His best advice, good then and better now, is keep an eye out for Ratty and Mole and Badger on the river, and a sharp watch for stoats and weasels.

And always keep an ear open for the sound of a knock on your door toward dawn.

It may be hobbits.

Armageddon and Cronies

It never looks like much, Armageddon.

It usually slips in about halfway through the film innocently enough, and you never take much notice until it's at the door, ten feet high and pissed. I never thought much about it, other than it was a good yarn from the Bible, but I was always on the lookout for guys looking like skeletons riding horses that were on fire.

Life isn't always like that.

What you get is Sky Riders suddenly appearing over the horizon, or A-bomb tests somewhere in the desert, and then maybe a war or two sprinkled in.

There's always one more Armageddon.

I saw it coming the way they were pumping water out of the great underground river that runs under the High Plains where I grew up. It wasn't anything special at the time, and it made the breadbasket of America look green and lush, full of the food that would feed the world. It wasn't anything out of the ordinary for the times to have someone standing out in a cotton field to move the row marker so the pilot of the spray plane could turn and wheel to hop the power lines and swoop back down on another pass, loosing the chemical concoctions that were supposed to kill the boll weevil that would destroy the cotton. They tried the same thing with bigger planes dumping Dow Chemical's Agent Orange on large tracts of real estate in Viet Nam, which was also full of other living things.

It was done evenly, like a storm at sea. Everyone got it, no matter whose side they were on. That was a strange thing, and it gets even stranger as time goes on. Admiral Zumwalt was commander of all naval personnel back then, which included his son, who died of complications brought on by Agent Orange.

Now I read that the Admiral has been "on the ground" in Viet Nam again. Not looking at satellite photos, or reading reports, but on the ground. He even had a meeting with General Giap, who gave the French Dien Bien Phu and masterminded the Tet Offensive in 1968.

If you could call it masterminding.

They had a funny way of waging a war, those fellows. It cost him thousands upon thousands of his own troops. It was like stopping a train by ordering people to lie down on the track.

General Giap was old then, and who knows what twisted things had happened to him to make him what he was, which was smart, with a good eye to read his enemies. He knew by watching the news that even a crushing defeat of his armies would cause the American public to demand a withdrawal from the Republic of South Vietnam.

The boll weevil got stronger and kept on eating the tasty cotton plants, and the same thing happened in Indo-China. Human beings suffered whether they were designated enemies or not. When the lead-slinging is over, everyone dies. The chemical rain poured down on both sides in a monsoon of death straight out of Armageddon.

Now, years later, I read that a rare and unknown sort of animal has been discovered far back in the damaged jungles in the highlands of Viet Nam. Like the hearty boll weevil, this animal and his cousins grew stronger from the assault on them and now flourish where nothing was supposed to be left alive.

I like the bigness of nature. No matter what mankind comes up with to throw her off track, she just rolls on.

They will let you in to see Trinity Site in the New Mexico desert once a year, and it catches one's eye that the bomb blast turned sand to glass where they tested their first efforts. The area around where the Sky Riders crashed has a pattern very similar.

Armageddon and its cronies.

The Admiral and General Giap, and the onetime Secretary

of Defense, Robert McNamara, have had their meetings, eying each other from vast distances of time and space, their lives tied up inextricably, marveling at the spectacle. President Johnson is dead, and if karmic law can be read right, doing his time paying off his crimes. The warp and weave of it staggers the imagination and just flows on, sweeping everyone up, all in perfect order. Even in Armageddon, the law grinds fine.

At last count, there were still roughly 300,000 Vietnamese soldiers missing in action, and at least a million deaths among the population in general.

They were the victors.

I think of my own small section of that war, without the benefit of an overview, touched by only those close to me, and on my watch. It's easier in some ways to look at it like that, if you can survive long enough. Tales of Armageddon only muddle the stew.

The saying went, "We were winning the war when I came home." That was another odd twist. Henry Kissinger and Richard M. Nixon gave us an "honorable peace," which led to a pull-out, and then as time went on, the North came south. Pondering things like that is good for the Armageddon file, thinking on who is doing what to whom. Living long is good revenge, because you begin to see that everything falls with an even hand. Not as much fun as the boys on flaming horses sweeping through town torching everything and everyone who has done something bad, but it's a lot more just.

Spray the boll weevil, and he will grow strong, eat more, and be immune to everything you throw at him. Slay your enemy, and he will rise from the paddies and jungles and rain fire and brimstone on you, killing himself in the process.

Carry hardware and die by it.

My friend Jackie marked rows for the spray planes to treat, and he never had kids and died of what has come to be known as High Plains cancer. In the business of gunfighters, you die of lead poisoning.

Boots on.

The Admiral and the General and the Secretary sat down to talk in a field of death, blooming with the spent flowers of young and old alike, silent as a shark's breath on the bottom of the sea.

And now I open my Sunday paper to the travel section and see that Viet Nam is being hawked as a new, très chic destination. "An out-of-the-way treat for the adventurous traveler."

I always liked the idea that you get back ten-fold whatever you're putting out. Life on the Road begins to spring things like that on you.

You walk every mile of the way, once you've found it, and the law does grind fine.

It's the only thing that makes sense in this circus of a world we live in. When you stop to think what that means, it takes the burr out from under your saddle blanket and makes everything a little more bearable.

I watched with my pals as soldiers from our unit pulled an old man and his young grandson out of the back of a building that had been shelled when Tet was running the hottest, and he patted our arms over and over, thanking us. We got his granddaughter out from under the rubble next. She had delivered a baby in the midst of all the excitement. It was covered with blood and caked with mud, but alive and healthy, dropped into the middle of a maelstrom that blew everything before it like leaves in a fiery wind.

I carry that image in my mind now, the frightened young woman with her newborn son, sitting in the wreckage of the war that surrounded her, holding that new life to her breast, protecting him with her frail, trembling body.

A flicker of light in the darkness of war, a splinter of love in the heart of hatred, like Pete Seeger's inscription on his banjo: "This machine surrounds hate and forces it to surrender." Right on, my brother, right on.

My friends who were there that day are mostly gone, carried

away all those years ago in that exotic, tropical land, far from all they knew. Carey Anthony was one of them who died among strangers, a young man from Arkansas, with an honest heart who would help anyone who asked him. A man who did not question your motives but gave of himself freely, in a simple, humble way.

The war shot him full of holes for his trouble, and I walk around in my life getting older and slower, wondering what would have become of him and all the others like him. I have stood before the Wall in Washington and seen my face reflected back from the black stone, felt the healing grace of seeing the lines upon lines of names, and touched the panels, 35 and 36E, where my old compadres reside, close to each other forever. I felt a cold wind blow through my bones then and wished the old wish, that I had died with them, so that I could be there, safe and warm, beyond the notion of guilt or justification.

My friend Brewin says no matter how many times you go to the Memorial, there is always another new strand of pain and release and tears. I thought about that on Armistice Day in 1992 as I watched the Indian Nations who lost sons perform in full ceremonial dress, dancing their cleansing dance and their warrior's dance in honor of all those who had gone away to the war and did not return. I remembered Jimmy Begay, a Navajo who was in our platoon in basic training, a shy young man with high cheekbones and strong legs. He almost killed all of us on training marches, out in that desert near where they fired off the first A-bomb, because he never tired. Our D.I.s would always say we'd stop when the Indian stopped.

Only he never did.

I wonder if he's walking now? Or is it his ghost walking?

I could use a five-minute break and a smoke.

Armageddon is a tiring business, when you're on the Road.

The Old Dime Box Theory

I used to lie awake in the hooch on Tent City Bravo and wonder why it was that someone had named a town Old Dime Box.

The question was good for taking your mind off the war, which was no easy task, as it was around you always, waiting to rear up and bite. It had teeth, and was invisible as well, so it did the job of filling up the hours with a low-grade sense of boredom and dread all rolled into one. The girls in the beautiful silk Áo dàis relieved some of that, but only in small spurts, and then they lent another strand to the warp and weave of Viet Nam, and that was the unspeakable romantic sadness which is at the heart of all wars. It is a time that never was, beyond the outside eaves of the human heart. It is horrible and haunting at once. While you are in the midst of it, you know it will end, which makes you sad. Years later, you look back with something more than sadness, a bittersweet longing, for the fire burns all alike, the lie and the liar, the veneer stripped away, until nothing is left in the end but that pure agony and grief and a wildness that is never found anywhere else. It is at once total freedom and the worst nightmare of confinement, more addicting than the most powerful drugs known to man.

It is power and powerlessness, everything precious that is life and the worst of all emptiness that comes with the death of a living soul.

The irony is that it is usually kicked off by some old farts somewhere deciding to be offended by the fact that no one is paying enough attention to the way they are controlling things. It ends with a blazing 122 mm. rocket round as a good punctuation mark.

Young men end up dying for some order given by leaders

who are twelve thousand miles away and don't have to dodge the end-table-size chunks of hot metal that get flung around when the thing goes off. I do believe in the Law, though, and I know that what goes around comes around, and that everything will fall into perfect order.

And in that perfect order, there were many late nights in the bunker behind the hooch spent wondering about everything, listening to the rocket and mortar rounds whomp-whomp-whomp their odd walk around the perimeter. It always ended the same, with no easily worded solutions.

Just like the war.

We hoped that somebody somewhere knew what the hell was going on and was working to make it all right.

Which was in a way exactly like trying to untie the knot of why Old Dime Box got that name. A friend suggested that it referred to a whore who had gotten old but kept her sense of humor, that she had gone into retirement in that part of Texas and named the town Old Dime Box as a sort of kindly reminder of her past glory. I've always tended to go along with that version, although there was another story I heard once, I can't remember exactly where, that had to do with a Texas Ranger's story about chasing a bunch of renegade Comanches through that part of the country and getting bushwhacked near the present site of Old Dime Box. When he was found two days later, he kept repeating something over and over. His friend, leaning down to try to hear his dying partner's words, couldn't make out much of anything. What his mortally wounded pal had been saying was that he had arrows in his whole damn back.

The man thought it was something about an old dime box, maybe something he wanted given to his next of kin.

Old Dime Box. Named by the misunderstood dying words of a Texas Ranger.

The town has been showing up on maps marked with blue lines, which indicate out-of-the-way, little-used roads, good for motorcycles and people who don't want to drive Interstates.

To protect itself, Old Dime Box has started to spin yarns to keep people from wanting to come there. It reminds me of a bumper sticker I saw years ago in Oregon: "Don't Californicate Oregon." Sentiments that have deep roots, which come out when a familiar place is threatened with being overrun by rank strangers.

It would take a dedicated stranger to move to and stay in Old Dime Box.

It didn't take too much study to see that the Vietnamese had been trying to run off everyone who had decided that they would move in and use the natural resources and exploit the beauty of the country as they saw fit.

Charlie Norton felt the same way about people moving in too close to him out in Chihuahua. Fort Hancock was about a hundred people too many for Charlie, who preferred spending time out by himself with just his pony for company. He'd do that for days at a time, until his sister would get worried about him and send one of his hands off to fetch him home to sit at her breakfast table for a meal or two. He was polite, and did his family duty, then he'd be gone again, out where he could breathe.

I asked Charlie about Old Dime Box while we were coming home from checking his herd across the border one afternoon, and he rode for a long time in silence, thinking about it. Working cowboys have a way of thinking about things, and are in such a habit of doing it, they may go for days before they answer.

"Same thing with Union Band," he said finally, just as we were pulling up in front of Al's bar. "Hell of a sign. Union Band Cemetery."

That was another town that crept up on the imagination and kept your gears turning. There was a ream of towns in Viet Nam that would do that. There was one that sounded like Bear Cat, but it was spelled differently. Two Duck was what we called the watch-rat that lived in our bunker, although it looked like Tu Duc in Vietnamese.

I liked the way it sounded better, and the idea that it made some sense.

No Pistols and No Spitting wasn't the name of a place but a sign I saw in a Best Western Motel in Laramie once. Seems like they had some trouble with rodeo hands shooting and spitting in the rooms for a while. Charlie laughed a lot about that one.

Adobe Walls.

Has a ring to it, and describes exactly what it was, out on the Llano Estacado, back when the XIT ranch was up and running and Old Tascosa was a hot little town thriving on the business of cattlemen and those who followed them. Drew a lot of colorful characters, and made the history books fairly hum with lively stories about the doings of those gents and ladies back when.

Viet Nam.

Soft sounds, but packing a punch. Rainbows and razor blades, firestorm and revelations. Raises a vast array of the wildest sort of emotions all over again just to hear it spoken.

Dead Horse Flats was another favorite on those old maps of New Mexico, and Bottomless Lakes says just what it means. They might be able to measure the depth of those lakes now, but it is a soulless venture that is sure to deaden the heart, probably the reason the world has come unstuck in time and more and more pages of the newspapers are filled with dreadful catastrophes. Chief George, who lived down the road from me in Fort Hancock, had a theory that the reason it was all happening was that the Highway Patrol arrested him for drunken bicycle riding on the Interstate and kept him in jail for a week, so he wasn't able to get back home to do the necessary sand painting that would help put the world back in balance.

His uncle, Chief Saul, was the tribal sand-painter before him. He died a few weeks before they set off the A-bomb in the desert a hundred and fifty miles up the road.

Things might have been different if the old man had lived, insisted Chief George. Charlie was of the same opinion and talked about the Big Skid. Mooch Crane used to say it was the Overtow getting active. Stay close to a tree or house, he always warned. You never know when you might need to get grounded, to avoid being carried away.

It's called hitting the ditch, in common terms, out in West Texas, when you lose control of your automobile and do an endo, or end-for-end. Ass-for-tip is what Charlie called it, describing what happens to a horse in that same situation, who might step in a gopher hole at a full run. Coming off the Road in a high-speed wobble, or with a blowout, has the same effect, sometimes to the tune of cashing in your chips, having to get back into another game at a later date.

John Martinez explained it to me not long ago. He was finishing up applying the robin's-egg-blue paint to the roof on my verandah as I sat writing on this.

"The blue is good for keeping the evil spirits away," he said, smiling his wry smile as he brushed. "Also for sure keeps away the mud daubers."

I like simple reads on the most mystifying sort of things. When I think about how completely simple it all is, I wonder how any of us ever got this far without a better road map.

But once you ask one question, you're sunk, and begin to ponder things like why any of it is going on, and where our part is in the grand scheme of things.

Or as Arty wanted to know, where's the door?

I do know this. If you have a blue roof on your porch, you can maybe dodge the evil spirits that are trying to keep you away from the Road, and you won't have mud daubers to worry with while you're reflecting on the other clues or trying to get your directions and regroup.

The Old Dime Box Theory, in effect.

A Road Song

I was sitting in a roadside cafe once outside Banning, California, and heard probably the second best advice I've ever heard. The first best was from my old First Sergeant, which went, "Do the best you can, be very careful, and keep a fresh round in the chamber."

Straight and to the point. In this day and age, it's hard to get concrete information that you can count on.

The woman was in her mid-forties, bleached blonde, and had just called me "Hon" when she refilled my coffee. She was talking to her friend behind the counter as she walked by me, and I caught the tail end of the conversation.

It has stuck with me.

"Just you tell that cowboy he can't wear his spurs in my house, 'cause I got a waterbed."

A rule to be remembered. No spurs in a waterbed.

That was the beginning of a road trip from Venice to the Gulf Coast, when I was looking for an exit from the Hotel California. You can leave, but you can't ever check out. I crossed the Colorado River at Blythe many times, thinking I had made good my escape, only to be reeled back in.

1 knew 1 was in trouble when I started to miss the smog that hung over L.A. as I was coming back in, burning to see the Pacific out at the end of Interstate 10, where it ends at the pier in Santa Monica.

There was nothing for it but to yo-yo out and back.

If you don't do the homework, you never get the grade. It gave meaning to a life spent in endless hours on the road, in my car or on a bike, looking at this country from the quiet island of that aloneness a solitary driver has.

My last trip comes to mind, where I'm back outside

Deming again, watching a rolling dark cloud come slowly over the mountains to the west and east, promising rough weather. The constant on any road trip is wondering about the weather.

The same can be said for being on the Road. You can depend on it to be undependable, whether you're coming or going.

Charlie Norton is out somewhere to the south and east of Deming, in that bigness he called his range, watching out over cowboys and their herds. I always stop by to see him at the cemetery in Fort Hancock, not because he's there, but that's where the phone booth is to call the Big Guy. Standing in that rocky little plot, it's easy to imagine Charlie free across the river, where you can see all the way to the top of the sky without getting a bump on your eye.

For my next trip, I have a new story for Charlie, about an unfired clay pot full of the ashes of a brother, and outlaw acts that always tickled him. Not banditry, which is another thing altogether, and what we mostly have now.

Bandits will kill you for nothing and have no code.

An outlaw is honorable, and follows a code, and will help women and children. You don't see many of that breed anymore.

This story took place on the Santa Catalina ferry and involves a foreigner and her dog and a nice young man who was informed that an illegal act was going to take place, and when he found out what it was, he chose to go along.

My wife's brother died in September 1990 of AIDS, and after cremation, had been waiting patiently at his house for a memorial service. One thing led to another, and a quilt was made and taken to Washington to be put with all the other panels, but nothing happened about the scattering of his ashes. Every time something was set up, one or another of his old friends couldn't make the date. Finally, in a desperate act, my wife and her sister flew to L.A. and took their brother for his last outing, slipping him over the side of the ferry on the way out to Catalina.

She told me that when the unfired clay pot Nick was in hit

the water, a rainbow appeared in the spray and stayed visible for the longest time.

As good an epitaph as you'll ever likely hear about.

I am a man who takes signs seriously, and that one put a catch in my throat when she told me. Taps being played does that to me, or the thought of Charlie being buried somewhere out in Chihuahua. Vikings burning their dead in their ships, or the Native Americans burying their own in the sky.

It's good to imagine the end of the story before you get to it, because you're going to be short-changed if you don't have some say-so in one of the more important acts in the play. There wouldn't be anything more galling than to be stuck in a box in a bone orchard while some stranger read your last scene for you.

It would be hard to one-up Charlie Norton, but I've heard some good swan songs in the past year or so, one of which is right up there with W.C. Fields and Barrymore. That was a classic coda to a wild Hollywood story, with Barrymore's friends kidnapping the body out of the funeral home and dragging him around to all the nightspots in town. Then there was one of Nick's friends who died and ended up on a chaise lounge in a tuxedo while a video he had made for his wake played to the gathering.

Charlie Norton hated company, and so was taken out to where his favorite old cowponies were left, which was perfect. He had described a perfect tombstone as being made up of your own bones, left to be picked clean by buzzards and coyotes. You become your own marker.

Ship graveyards dot the oceans of the world, When you see the eerie shots of those dark, watery graves, you get the same sensation of being somewhere you shouldn't be, of opening some secret door that is never meant to be opened. I would be riled to think that someone would dig Charlie up, if they were to stumble across where he's buried out in Chihuahua. I get riled up when I hear of Indian gravesites being plundered for pottery or relics to sell in high-dollar joints in Taos or Santa Fe.

Mooch Crane found the grave of an early settler on a remote part of one of his sections of land and had Calvin Blaine come out and erect a black wrought-iron fence around it so his hands wouldn't plough it over when they went to replant the winter wheat.

It's still an odd sight to see the weathered fence out in that field. No one knew a name to put on it, so it simply reads, "R.I.P. A Soul Known Only to God," and the year and month it was put up.

I like to watch the videos of wailing Arab women and men firing off their weapons into the air to grieve over the loss of a loved one. There isn't anything more spiritually soothing than that. It seems so much more civilized than tiptoeing around in a funeral home, listening to organ music and speaking in hushed tones about the deceased.

I would prefer a lot of my rowdy friends dressed to ride, and maybe my old favorite rock-'n'-roll from the fifties and sixties. A run to the Wall, where they could leave my ashes to be picked up by the Park Service.

Rolling thunder.

A send-off.

The Sky Riders must have had their own version of a send-off when they came a cropper out in the desert, accompanied by thunder and lightning and whatever might have exploded in their ship.

It would be a good way to go.

More Road signs.

Like Old Man Autry in the small hometown I grew up in, always watching for the arrival of the Colonel. He'd been gassed in World War I and never was the same. He would roam around with a map in his hat, and explain to you carefully where you were, and how to get where you needed to be. We'd know what to do when the Colonel came. Old Man Autry would sit at O.C. Pullem's Gulf service station where I was pumping gas on long summer afternoons in the mid-1950s, drinking a big orange soda pop with peanuts in it, rambling on about things I didn't understand. I liked the old man and never minded when he came.

Sheriff Lovelace had a different problem with him when he insisted on stopping big rigs on the highway to direct them. That almost proved fatal on more than one occasion, and Old Man Autry always promised to be good. Then he would hear the old voice inside and think he was back in France in 1918, and he had to answer the call.

My grandfather and his friends took up a collection to bury the old man when he finally died, and there's a stone in the cemetery there with his name and service number.

When I think back now on those long summer afternoons, I vaguely remember the old man telling me about the funny lights he'd seen out over the countryside toward the west. This wasn't long after the crash outside Roswell, and everyone thought he'd heard someone talking about it.

He and the Colonel had shown them where to go.

I expect I nodded and smiled and bought him another big orange and more peanuts, thinking about Saturday night and the girl I was going to ask out on a date.

Not many people showed up for his funeral, and the town went on. It was a lot less interesting those last few summers I worked at the service station without the old man. Times were changing, and I was leaving home to go away to school. What had been my world there was being replaced with bigger dreams and broader horizons.

Now I return there on my travels and see the Road signs and wonder at the marvel of it. Being so close to the mystery sometimes is the perfect cover. If you want to keep a secret, broadcast it.

No one looks for something that is common knowledge.

I can almost hear the sounds of those big Trans-Con rigs now, going slowly through the gears, and Old Man Autry getting up from the metal lawn chair, saying he'd better get to work. He'd take that map from his hatband and step smartly out to the highway, ready for business.

I shared big orange drinks and peanuts with a man who may have had a map to the Sacred Mountain, and I never once asked for directions.

He had the bluest eyes, almost no color, they were so light.

When he looked directly at you, it was like seeing the young man he was in 1918, only now he was in an old body. Charlie Norton told me about an old Mexican man who lived on his spread in Chihuahua who had been with Pancho Villa. Something had happened to him in the revolution, and he spoke to trees and rocks and lived by himself. Everyone left him food and clothing, but people were afraid of him.

Charlie's answer to why he had dealings with the old man was simple. "He was a good hand at branding," he explained. "He knew how to ride."

That was the old man who showed Charlie the Indian holy grounds and where the buried gold was hidden and told him about all the visitors he had at his little shack

That was years before the Sky Riders crashed in 1947.

When I pressed Charlie about what the old man said about his visitors, he snorted one of his little laughs. "He never said they were green."

We're still waiting for the Colonel.

One of the best things about travel is that you get to sit down somewhere along the way and look at all the postcards from the places you've been. From a distance, it all comes so much clearer, and you wonder how you ever missed the point.

Road songs are a lot sweeter when you have time to listen to them.

A Grave Next to Buddy Holly

I knew it was the end of the road when they pulled my mother from the hole in the City of Lubbock Cemetery, where she rested not far from Buddy Holly, and reburied her in my small hometown, next to her mother and father and her little sister, who was killed in a car wreck in the New Mexican desert when she was three.

It happened just outside Alamogordo, near the Trinity site.

That was in 1925, before people on earth knew about things to come, like Sky Riders or A-bombs. The land was full of older, more important powers, and Al Rivera, my good desert-rat compadre from my outlaw days in Chihuahua who ran the bar called Bar with his wife Janie, took me to some places out in those stark desert mountains which had been the sea floor once that made the hair on the back of my neck stand up. Charlie Norton had his chambered nautilus and knew about the Indian holy grounds. Al had found more than one place out along certain mesas that was long and flat and looked like it could have been shaped as some sort of landing field. Upon closer inspection, it seemed meant for some type of aircraft that were far beyond anything in existence then.

Then there were the strange petroglyphs, in a rough and primitive scrawl, depicting flying objects, and alongside them what appeared to be symbols carved by laser or something similar.

I asked Al if he had ever reported those sites to the authorities. He laughed and pointed to his reconditioned arm and leg, which had been put back together after his Navy PBY was shot down off Guadalcanal. He'd been a radio-operator-gunner and was thrown into the forward flight compartment when the pilot ditched the craft, and spent months in the hospital, first in California, then at Fort Bliss.

"That's what happens when you report something to them. Bandits, I said, and the next thing I know, we're in the drink, and I can't move."

So the sites are still there, still undiscovered by anyone but desert rats roaming around, or now the marijuana farmers who have taken over the territory.

Those spots are still undisturbed, but not so where my mother was first laid to rest.

It's a serious thing when they dig you up and move you somewhere else. It had been an uneasy peace between my mother and me for all the years we had been on the planet together, and I guess it was an unexpected shock when she got out. Just cashed out quietly before I could get there, although I had seen her not a week before. Sometimes I think mothers do those sorts of things just to prove who's still boss.

She never said much in regard to anything personal about her life, like why she divorced my father or what made her so unhappy, and I spent all my life away from her, making contact here and there along the way. My father lived thirty miles away in Portales, that peanut town in the middle of the great sand dunes where the Clovis people roamed, where they had begun to find all sorts of leftovers from an ancient society, a track in the wilderness that made it fairly clear that there was probably more than one reason for the Sky Riders to be in that neck of the New Mexico desert.

On that bike trip past Roswell in the electrical storm, I had stopped by to see the headstone where my father was buried. Three men sat drinking in the back of a pickup on that Sunday afternoon, watching as I put my side stand down and took my helmet off. One of them came over.

"Nice ride," he said, admiring the Harley.

"Thanks. I'm looking for my dad." The man looked startled till I went on. "He's buried out here somewhere. He died in 1965."

"Harry," the man shouted back to his friends in the truck.

177

"Where's the plot for 1965?" That was such a good question, I thought about it and didn't hear his friend's answer. In 1965 my ex-wife was in the process of getting out of town, and I was holed up at my friend Mickey Byrd's house, exploring the relief I could find in a bottle of Cutty Sark scotch. The world was an explosive place at that time. Everything was on the point of a change so profound it wouldn't be recognizable to anyone from any generation. I sat on the couch at Mickey's house sipping my scotch with my leather elbow patches on my sportcoat, listening to the Beatles and wondering where the wind would blow next. I needn't have worried. There was a hurricane brewing up outside the window, and it would only be a matter of a few more months before I would look out over the landscape and see nothing but wreckage and debris from the remains of my old world.

Bleak ocean, everything that was before was gone. The pages of the old script were torn out, and a new unknown direction appeared.

Around that time, my mother called and came by Mickey's every day, knocking loudly. I was inside, but I didn't want to face her, so I simply lay on the couch until she went away. She left a note in the mailbox about my father's death and wrote down the day and time of the funeral in Portales, where they were famous for their peanuts. She ended up sending the police to the door to make sure the message was delivered. That was on the morning of the day of his burial.

I dressed and drove the 120 miles and arrived after the services at the cemetery. I spent an hour or so at the wake, and my father's new wife drove me out so I could see the grave. I threw a luck-piece in and muttered a good-bye, then drove away. Twenty-nine years later, the man in the back of the pickup shouted back that 1965 was just across the fence from where we were standing.

Bone orchards are strange, otherworldly places, and the stones where I was walking all spoke of a time passed, both

178

in distance and style. I kept an eye on my bike as I walked in the midafternoon sunlight, down past the markers for my Uncle Jake and my Grandmother Gongy, and then there he was. Samuel Nathaniel Hancock. The wind in the trees was as soft as a bird's wing passing, and I could hear the insects singing. Cars passed by on the road, and when I looked, the three men were back in the bed of the pickup, drinking their beer and watching me with little interest. I sat down in front of the marker, said hello, thanked my father for bringing me into the world, and said I was sorry that I hadn't gotten to know him better. We both had lost out, I offered.

For no apparent reason, I suddenly realized I was crying. I didn't want to go back to my bike in front of the men in the truck so I sat there a little longer until I could keep a calm face and wandered away, wondering why that felt so bad.

The good thing about Harley-Davidsons is that they fill up a space with their being, and when you light them off, they make a wonderful thunder. Inside my helmet I was crying again, but the men couldn't see. As I rode away, I shouted another good-bye back over my shoulder, with the promise that I'd be by to see him next time.

That's the line I use every time I leave someone. I used it when I left my grandparents' house. and upon leaving my friends for the Army, and when I shipped out for Viet Nam, and when I left to fly home to The World. I still use it now in airports or cabs, or waving to someone driving or riding away, or when I'm on the road.

I had told my mother that, the last time I saw her alive, and the next time was in the funeral home in Lubbock, where they took her out to the City of Lubbock Cemetery and lowered her down into a grave not far from the legendary Buddy Holly, the kid with the black horn-rims who skyrocketed to rock-'n'-roll fame, then died in a winter plane crash in a cornfield outside Clear Lake, Iowa, in 1959.

See you next time, I said when I left.

The Sky Riders would have told that to someone, wherever they were from, and there were sad hearts somewhere when they never returned. Like watching the black coffins at the morgue in Tan Son Nhut being loaded for return to the United States, each one returning to family and friends with what was left of a person who had died in a war. Some of the coffins had nothing in them but scraps of flesh, a bone, or a piece of meat. Some, like the kid on the sandbags, looked as though he'd just lain down to go to sleep.

See you next time.

The hole a person leaves in your life is a gaping one, and it takes some time to mend. Charles Whitehouse said he could do it by repairing your aura. He had a machine to take pictures of where the holes were, then he would patch them, like in the old days when you could patch an inner tube to fix a tire.

It would be nice to have it so easy.

Somewhere out about Tucson, it began to feel better, and I thought about my old trick knee when I was a kid. If I turned my foot wrong, part of the cartilage would slip up under my kneecap and lock it, causing extreme pain. The only relief was to straighten the leg, which was sheer agony, and then everything would pop back into place.

It was that kind of relief.

The bike rumbled on beneath me, and the country began to change again, rolling up toward Flagstaff and the Big Ditch.

I've heard of spots in the Grand Canyon where the Sky Riders would hide their craft when they were exploring Earth. During the building of Boulder Dam, there were endless accounts of unidentifiable objects found that no one could explain. Because no one could properly catalogue them, they simply finished the dam and flooded the area.

Now Lake Mead is a Sky Rider museum.

That's where my cousin Tommy, the one who took me on his Indian Chief, bought it driving his big speedboat.

See you next time, he said, and was gone.

I've seen a picture of me in front of him on the saddle of that bike, smiling out at the Kodak box camera. Behind us, slightly out of focus, is the lake, stretching out beyond. My cousin Byron is on his machine next to us, and just at the edge of the picture, my grandfather is standing with his arm on the shoulder of my grandmother.

We are all frozen in amber, wandering somewhere on the Road, looking into the future. I remembered it all and wondered then if my father had seen the Sky Riders, or what he thought if he did.

His new wife, who was a strange one, told me at the wake that he was from Aldebaran, and they had called him home.

Star Children, she said, have colonized the Cosmos to bring higher awareness and learning to the far-flung outposts that had lagged behind.

I thought of the three men in the pickup drinking beer and wondered if they knew there was a man from Aldebaran buried in their town. None of them was old enough to have known my father or any of his family. Other than me, they would never have touched any part of that past. It slides by, like the Colorado running into Lake Mead, passing and past, with deep secrets that begin to speak only if you are still long enough to listen.

See you next time, the river seems to say.

There were two Chinese elm trees in the front yard of the house where I grew up. I saw a picture once of my father holding me up on one of the limbs, his hat tilted back, revealing his handsome face. We're both looking at whoever was holding the camera with that half-expectant smile of something extremely wonderful that will be coming along any time now.

It must have been my mother who was taking the snapshot. I don't remember seeing any picture of her from that time, which seems odd. There are photos of my grandfather and me, and me with my grandmother and aunt, but none of my mother and me.

Charlie Norton would have described our relationship as a Mexican Standoff.

Two men across the table from each other with sawed-off 12 gauge scatterguns with double-ought buckshot loads.

Now my mother is buried next to her father and mother and little sister, and I have a photo of it, not from a Kodak box camera, but a new, improved 35 mm. autoloader.

No Buddy Holly, but she's not far from V. Scott Johnson, the doctor who delivered me, and just across the way is Calvin Blaine, who saw the White Buffalo one snowy night on the Llano Estacado.

She is a hundred miles closer to my father.

Even in death, the wanderer still moves, always coming closer to the moment of reunion with all our other fellow travelers.

See you next time, I'll say, when the snow and ice is gone from the prairie and I'm able to ride the Harley up to see where they've moved her.

It's only another hundred twenty miles west to the spot where the Sky Riders came down.

Star Children scattered like dust in the wind. See you next time.

About the Author

Niel Hancock was born January 8, 1941, in Clovis, New Mexico. He died of an aortic aneurysm on May 7, 2011, in Deming, New Mexico, on his way home from his yearly spring motorcycle trip on his beloved BMW, Sophia DeVille. Drafted into the Army during the Vietnam war, he served as an Army MP stationed in Saigon during the Tet offensive of 1968. As a writer, he was an early practitioner of High Fantasy in the wake of J.R.R. Tolkien, between 1977 and 1990 publishing three series of books, *The Circle of Light*, *The Wilderness of Four*, and *The Windameir Circle*, plus a stand-alone volume, *Dragon Winter*. They are "historical mythologies" reflecting his Buddhist spiritual values.

CPSIA information can be obtained
at www.ICGtesting.com
Printed in the USA
FFOW04n1605100915
16665FF